THE UNOFFICIAL CORONATION ST QUIZ BOOK

summersdale

CW00321887

THE ULTIMATE UNOFFICIAL *CORONATION STREET* QUIZ BOOK

Summersdale Publishers Ltd
46 West Street
Chichester
West Sussex
PO19 1RP
UK

www.summersdale.com

Printed and bound in Great Britain

ISBN: 978-1-84953-097-2

Substantial discounts on bulk quantities of Summersdale books are available to corporations, professional associations and other organisations. For details contact Summersdale Publishers by telephone: +44 (0) 1243 771107, fax: +44 (0) 1243 786300 or email: nicky@summersdale.com.

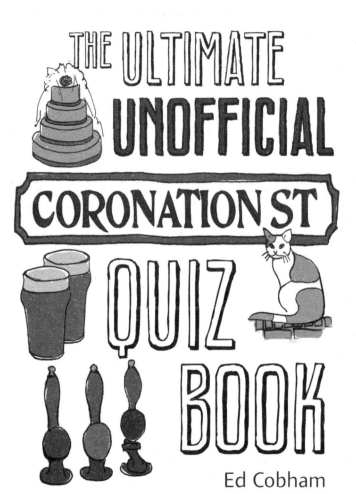

THE ULTIMATE UNOFFICIAL CORONATION ST QUIZ BOOK

Ed Cobham

CONTENTS

INTRODUCTION

As familiar as the lullabies your Mam used to sing, from the moment Eric Spear's iconic theme tune was first broadcast, *Corrie* was a hit. But having declared it 'doomed from the outset with its grim scene of terraced houses and smoking chimneys', former TV critic Ken Irwin must be eating his words in a super-sized portion. Not since the Hartford Women's Friday Club announced that electricity, though an interesting experiment, was too dangerous to be of practical use, has a prediction been so wide of the mark.

Having kept you captivated for the past half century with their tragedies and dramas, for many it's *Corrie's* down-to-earth humour that is the show's ultimate appeal. But where there is light so too is there shade, as shown in brilliantly written scenes that are performed with heartbreaking poignancy: Hilda Ogden sobbing over her late husband's specs; Sally Webster breaking the news of her breast cancer to husband Kevin; Peter Barlow's decline into alcoholism. These compelling storylines deal with subjects we can all identify with (give or take the activities of the occasional mass-murdering financial advisor!).

But 50 years is a long time, and recalling the details of every episode would be a challenge for even the most dedicated follower of *Corrie*. But what wonderful trips down memory lane – or in this case the Street – one would have in the attempt, which is where this book comes in. If you're a Barlow buff, a Duckworth devotee or a Rovers know-all, prepare to reminisce while testing yourself on all things Weatherfield. Maybe throw your own Rovers pub quiz? OK, so you won't get to share all the Street gossip with Norris, or half a bitter and the Gazette crossword with Ken, but for pure *Corrie* escapism it's the next best thing. As Ena Sharples said before she dropped off t'hooks, 'There've been times when Elsie Tanner's life's kept mine going. I've a lot to thank her for.'

A note about the answers

While some female characters have always had the same surname on the show, others have proudly taken their husbands' monikers, sometimes on more than one occasion. Characters are referred to in questions and answers with the surname in use at the time of publication or the last name used when they left the show, unless the question or answer refers to a specific time period.

CORRIE THROUGH THE YEARS

1960s

1. Who was fined £1.00 in court for selling firelighters after 7.30 p.m.?

2. Who attended a Ban the Bomb march, much to his father's fury?

3. Who put a notice in the local paper threatening legal action to those spreading gossip about her?

4. Who dated Eunice Bond, an exotic dancer who used a snake in her act?

5. To whom did Annie Walker say beauty queen Philippa Scope was too common to marry?

6. Why did Ena write to the Duke of Edinburgh?

7. Which couple celebrated their silver wedding anniversary in 1962?

8. Who took Elsie to the Federation of Master Builders' dance in 1963?

9. Who fell down the stairs while cleaning at the Viaduct Sporting Club?

10. Who became the Rovers cleaner in 1964?

11. What did Stan Ogden dig up in Albert Tatlock's backyard?

12. Who brewed beer and kept it in Minnie's house, pretending that it was a tonic?

13. Who became manageress of Gamma Garments in 1965?

14. Who knocked Ken out in a Rovers brawl in 1965?

15. Who did Lucille Hewitt fall in love with in 1966?

16. What did Annie Walker want to change the Rovers name to in 1966?

17. What inspired Annie to re-christen the pub?

18. In which month of which year was the first colour episode of *Corrie* screened?

19. What did Albert Tatlock accuse Miklos Zadic of stealing from him?

20. Who upset Ena by hanging out her washing on 'the Lord's day'?

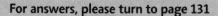

For answers, please turn to page 131

1970s

1. Irma Barlow and who became flatmates in 1970?

2. Which *Corrie* barmaid did ex-convict Keith Lucas stalk, culminating in him sneaking into her house?

3. Who 'discovered' a talented child harmonium player and persuaded the head of the local music college to award the lad a scholarship?

4. Which character first appeared in 1971 for what was meant to be a single episode, but proved so popular that she later joined the full-time cast?

5. What did drayman Arthur Burrows do in 1971 that got Annie Walker into trouble?

6. Who applied to be the Barlow twins' nanny but was turned down by Ken, who believed that the lady in question would mollycoddle them?

7. Who splashed out on a cocktail bar for their house after a win on the Premium Bonds?

8. Which of Ken Barlow's women made her first appearance in 1972?

9. Arriving in 1972 (although she had made a one-off appearance in the 60s), which character claimed to have once had a trifle named after her by a Labour Club?

10 What business did Dave Smith sell to Benny Lewis?

11 In the 1972 Christmas Day entertainment at the Rovers, who performed as Carmen Miranda?

12 Who got a job at The Kabin in 1973, despite having an attack of hiccups during the interview?

13 What did Alan Howard organise in 1973, resulting in a schoolboy, Mark Hillkirk, needing a skin graft?

14 Who collapsed during a sponsored swim in 1973?

15 What kind of race did The Flying Horse challenge the Rovers to in 1978?

16 Who did Martin Downes think looked so cheap that he left without introducing himself when he visited the Rovers in 1974?

17 Who, together with Tricia Hopkins, enrolled on the Jet Girl Agency modelling course in 1975?

18 In 1976, who sold her corset business and left the cobbles to go and run a country club?

19 Who bought the corner shop from Gordon Clegg in 1976?

20 Who started a petition to bring back hanging in 1978?

For answers, please turn to page 131

1980s

1. Who walked out on her husband in 1980 because she was fed up with being treated like a housekeeper?

2. Who turned up on Gail Tilsley's doorstep sporting a black eye in 1981?

3. Who held Emily Swain hostage, claiming that God had told him that they should commit suicide together?

4. At which couple's engagement party in 1982 was the Rovers piano pushed out onto the Street, with the police arriving shortly afterwards?

5. Who did Mavis collaborate with to pen a short story entitled *A Night to Forget*?

6. Why did the *Daily Mail* hire the Old Trafford scoreboard in 1983?

7. Who was sacked from the show in 1983 for flogging his life story to the press, an act that breached the terms of the actor's contract?

8. Who had her smalls pinched from the washing line in 1984?

9. Who became Hilda's lodger in 1985?

10. Designed by Christine Millward, what item of clothing did Mike Baldwin's factory start manufacturing in 1985?

11. Who stormed into Mike's factory in 1986 and punched him?

12. Who loaned Bet Lynch the money to buy the tenancy of the Rovers from the brewery?

13. Who was accused of racism in 1988 when he wouldn't let his flat to Shirley Armitage because she was black?

14. Who bought the garage after Brian Tilsley's death?

15. Who was Megan Morgan, and what did she do?

16. Who revealed that she had given birth to a son when she was just 16?

17. Who did Alma Sedgewick seduce by beating him at golf?

18. Whose wife threw him out on New Year's Eve 1989 for having an affair with his secretary?

19. Which pair travelled to London to witness the public wedding celebrations of Prince Charles and Lady Diana Spencer?

20. Which family moved into number 11 in 1989?

For answers, please turn to page 132

1990s

1. Which couple's first scene on the Street was filmed in front of visiting Prime Minister Margaret Thatcher?

2. Who sold his car to Curly Watts even though he knew it wasn't in good working order?

3. Who started skipping school and visiting arcades?

4. Who shaved off Kevin Webster's moustache at a party for a bet?

5. Who began sleeping in the stock room at Betterbuy because his wife had slung him out?

6. What did Phyllis Pearce win in 1990?

7. What happened when Phyllis raced to tell Percy Sugden about her win?

8. Initially written in as a character scheduled to appear for just a month, which actress was such a hit that she was brought back on a long-term contract?

9. Who in this decade claimed that his wife could 'find reasons why Mary and Joseph were unfit parents'?

10. What did Curly Watts spend £2,000 on in 1992?

11 Who had his lower leg amputated in 1992?

12 Which young character was rushed to Weatherfield General Hospital with a ruptured appendix in 1994?

13 Who fell in love with a Moroccan waiter in 1994?

14 Who inherited £240,000 from her parents' estate on her 18th birthday in 1995?

15 Who was held at gunpoint by Fraser Henderson's henchman Gerry Turner in 1997?

16 To whom was Tony Blair referring in 1998 when he asked the Home Secretary to intervene in the case of a *Corrie* character?

17 Encouraged by Ken Barlow, which teenager started writing articles for *Just 16* magazine?

18 Who was sacked for stealing knickers from Underworld before breaking into and squatting in Curly Watts' house?

19 Who moved out of the Street and was bound for Brighton in 1998?

20 Why did Spider dump his vegan girlfriend?

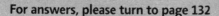

For answers, please turn to page 132

2000s

1. Which character's storyline put underage sex on the news agenda?

2. Who had sex with evil Jez Quigley in a bid to prevent him from carrying out a planned raid on the Rovers?

3. Whose sister began working as hairdresser at Audrey's salon and started dating Duggie Ferguson?

4. Who saved Paula Shipley's son from drowning and then found love with Paula?

5. How did Tyrone Dobbs take 'artistic' revenge on Les Battersby for taunting him for being illiterate?

6. Who fell for bookstore owner Anthony Stephens in 2000?

7. What was the name of Dev's ex-girlfriend who announced that Dev had promised to marry her, that she was expecting his child, and that she had tried to kill herself?

8. In 2002, who helped Joe Carter to take the factory from Mike Baldwin via a scam involving forged cheques for a non-existent company?

9. Which character was employed as a sonographer at Weatherfield General Hospital and held Maria Connor's hand when she had a stillborn son?

18

10. Which killer did Eileen Grimshaw date?

11. What did Eileen Grimshaw discover on her Dad, Colin's, 70th birthday?

12. Which character returned to the cobbles in 2008 after an absence of more than 40 years?

13. Who jilted Charlie Stubbs?

14. Who cruelly taunted Karen McDonald by calling her 'Barren Karen' when Karen couldn't conceive?

15. Who found a baby left on her doorstep on Christmas Day 2006?

16. Which character had emergency surgery as a result of an ectopic pregnancy in 2007?

17. In 2009, who was paid to kill Carla Connor but ended up getting a crack on the head with a weighty candlestick from her?

18. Who rowed with Roy Cropper over a colony of bats?

19. Which character sailed out of the Street for a while in 2009, embarking on a world cruise?

20. Who lost Simon Barlow in Blackpool in 2010?

For answers, please turn to page 133

19

WHO'S WHO?

Quiz One

1. Who played Vera Duckworth?

2. Who played entrepreneur Mike Baldwin?

3. Actor Craig Gazey was better known as which character?

4. Who played Jack Duckworth?

5. Which actress would *Corrie* fans know better as Molly Dobbs?

6. Who played the redoubtable Annie Walker?

7. Which Webster would you associate with actress Brooke Vincent?

8. The role of binman Trevor Dean was created by which actor?

9. Who played the legendary Hilda Ogden?

10. What is the name of the actor cast as *Corrie*'s Dev Alahan?

For answers, please turn to page 134

Quiz Two

1 Which actress would you associate with the character Sunita Alahan?

2 Anne Kirkbride was better known as which which long-running character?

3 Which actor was more familiar to *Corrie* fans as bigamist bookie and recovering alcoholic Peter Barlow?

4 Jane Danson was better known as which *Corrie* lady?

5 Samuel Aston was the actor behind which cute character?

6 If Katy Cavanagh was the actress, who was the character?

7 Julie Hesmondhalgh was more familiar as which character?

8 Sue Cleaver was better known as which *Corrie* matriarch?

9 Actor and singer Keith Duffy was known on the Street as which heartthrob?

10 Who was the actress behind the character of feisty Becky McDonald?

For answers, please turn to page 134

Quiz Three

1. Which mutton-dressed-as-lamb character would you associate with actress Beverley Callard?

2. Actress Barbara Knox was better known as which long-running character?

3. Who was the actor known to *Corrie* fans as Kirk Sutherland?

4. Simon Gregson was more familiar as which of Liz McDonald's sons?

5. Michelle Keegan was the actress behind which *Corrie* beauty?

6. If David Neilson was the actor, who was the quirky character?

7. Who was the actor known on the cobbles as garage mechanic Tyrone Dobbs?

8. Which actress was renowned for her role as the 'Good Christian Woman' that was the genteel Emily Bishop?

9. Who played crotchety Uncle Albert?

10. Who played bad boy Terry Duckworth?

For answers, please turn to page 134

Quiz Four

1. William Roache was eternally linked to which veteran character?

2. Which actress originally auditioned for the role of Hilda Ogden, but instead became the Street's Betty Williams?

3. Actress Anne Kirkbride was better known as which *Corrie* character?

4. Helen Worth was the actress linked to which Street lady?

5. Sue Nicholls was more familiar as which *Corrie* hairdresser?

6. Which actor was known to *Corrie* fans as Kevin Webster?

7. Who was the actress behind the character of Sally Webster?

8. How was Malcolm Hebden better known to *Corrie* viewers?

9. John Savident played which gregarious character?

10. Vicky Entwistle played which lairy lady?

For answers, please turn to page 134

Quiz Five

1. Who played unlucky-in-love Shelley Unwin?

2. Kate Ford was best known for her tricky antics as which *Corrie* miss?

3. Wendi Peters played which gob-on-a-stick character?

4. Which actress was best known as Sophie Webster?

5. Samuel Aston was associated with which *Corrie* kid?

6. Which character was played by Chris Oakes, Chris Cook and Paul Fox?

7. Owen Aaronovitch played which dastardly character in the late 90s?

8. Who played Rita's husband, Len Fairclough?

9. How was Betty Alberge known to *Corrie* viewers?

10. Peter Baldwin played which (mostly) comedy *Corrie* character?

For answers, please turn to page 134

Quiz Six

1. Pauline Fleming played which of Mike Baldwin's women?

2. Which effervescent lady was actress Jennie McAlpine better known as?

3. Who played gymslip mum Sarah Platt?

4. Who played Bev Unwin?

5. Rupert Hill played which character?

6. Helen Flanagan was better known as which *Corrie* babe?

7. If David Platt was the character, who was the actor?

8. Antony Cotton was the actor behind which camp character?

9. Who played Rita and Len Fairclough's foster daughter Sharon?

10. Which actor was better known on TV as hunky builder Jason Grimshaw?

For answers, please turn to page 135

27

Quiz Seven

1. Steven Arnold was better known as whom?

2. Which actress was known in Weatherfield as Claire Peacock?

3. Bruce Jones played which lovable rogue?

4. Who was behind the character of Hayley Cropper?

5. Who played barmaid Violet Wilson?

6. Bradley Walsh played which cockney *Corrie* cast member?

7. Who played machinist Kelly Crabtree?

8. Which actress was more familiar to *Corrie* viewers as Maria Connor?

9. Eric Potts played which foodie fella?

10. Debra Stephenson played whom?

For answers, please turn to page 135

HAPPY FAMILIES

The McDonalds

1   What was the name of Steve McDonald's twin brother?

2   At which number did the McDonald clan reside when they first arrived in the Street?

3   In 2007, Liz McDonald cheated on hubby Vernon with whom?

4   Who did Steve McDonald marry in 1995?

5   Why was Steve sent to prison in 1996?

6   In which year did Becky McDonald join the *Corrie* cast?

7   Which hairdresser gave both Jim and Steve McDonald more than just a short back and sides?

8   Who did Steve McDonald marry for a bet?

9   Whose christening did Karen McDonald gatecrash, hell-bent on wreaking havoc?

10 Who pushed Jim McDonald off scaffolding?

11 Which members of the McDonald clan went joyriding with a JCB, which culminated in them crashing into Alf's shop window?

12 Which McDonald became licensee of the Rovers in 2006?

13 Which McDonald served in the army?

14 Which McDonald went on holiday to Malta with Eileen Grimshaw?

15 While in Malta, what was odd about the holiday romance Steve had with Shania?

16 What was the name of the bookie that Liz enjoyed a relationship with in 2008?

17 Which McDonald once worked as a supermarket trainee?

18 With which McDonald twin did Tracy Barlow have a one-night-stand, resulting in her getting pregnant?

19 Who planted drugs on Becky McDonald?

20 Who beat up Vernon Tomlin on his wedding day?

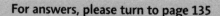

For answers, please turn to page 135

The Platts and the Tilsleys

1. What was Brenda Fearns' relationship to Bethany Platt?

2. Who was Sarah's father?

3. In which year did Adam Rickitt take over the role of Nicky Tilsley?

4. Who was Gail's father?

5. Who discovered Ivy Tilsley's diary in the attic of 5 Coronation Street and pretended to be 'channelling' Ivy?

6. Who was Ivy's first husband?

7. Which member of the Platt family had an affair with unhinged nurse Carmel Finnan?

8. What was the profession of Brian Tilsley?

9. Whose cousin did Gail's husband, con man and murderer Richard Hillman claim to be when he arrived in the Street?

10. As part of his dastardly plot, who did Richard Hillman try to make out had dementia?

11. Warren Jackson played which character?

12 What was the name of Gail's brother?

13 Why was there a question mark over Sarah's paternity?

14 Who was Ivy's second husband?

15 Which member of Gail's family offered to give a false testimony at Tracy Barlow's murder trial in return for sexual favours?

16 What was Gail's husband Joe McIntyre addicted to?

17 Who spent four months in a young offenders' institution?

18 Who pinched Jason Grimshaw from his then girlfriend Violet?

19 Who did Sarah jack in her studies for and move into a flat with?

20 Who did Ivy bequeath her house to on the proviso that the person concerned took her surname?

For answers, please turn to page 136

33

The Barlows

1. Which Barlow was killed in a car smash with his son in Australia in 1970?

2. With whom did Ken have a steamy affair in 1985?

3. In which year did Ken and Deirdre first marry?

4. How did Ida Barlow meet her maker in 1961?

5. Which Barlow moved to Wilmslow following a Premium Bond win of £5,000?

6. In 1997, which of Ken's women was found guilty of fraud and sentenced to 18 months in jail?

7. What was the name of the houseboat-dwelling floozy that Ken almost ran off with in 2009, and who played the role?

8. Who was the hairdresser mother of Ken's son Daniel?

9. Who did Susan Barlow marry in May 1986, much to her father's disgruntlement?

10. Who was the mother of Peter Barlow's son Simon?

11. To which Barlow did Samir Rachid donate a kidney, and why?

12 Who was Ken's razor-tongued mother-in-law?

13 For whose murder was Tracy Barlow imprisoned in 2007?

14 Which *Corrie* character died in Ken's arms, on the cobbles, in 2006?

15 Which schoolboy got a slap from Ken Barlow in 2002?

16 Who paid the bill for Deirdre's appeal when she was sent down?

17 Who did Peter Barlow marry – albeit bigamously – in July 2003?

18 The day before which royal couple did Ken and Deirdre remarry in 2005?

19 Which Barlow shared a prison cell with Gail in 2010?

20 Which Barlow fell asleep with a lit cigarette, resulting in a near-fatal fire in 2009?

For answers, please turn to page 136

The Windasses

1. Which Windass tried to scam fellow players on the Rover's darts team?

2. Which Windass started work at Roy's Rolls in 2009?

3. In the storyline that introduced them to the Street, who did the Windass clan refuse to pay for services rendered?

4. Whose house did Gary burgle in a set-up job by David Platt?

5. Who used Roy Cropper's account details at the cash and carry to buy fags and booze?

6. Which Windass hopped into bed with Rosie Webster on her birthday?

7. Which Windass went AWOL from the army in 2010?

8. Whose tools did Len and Gary Windass take, leaving the chap concerned unable to ply his trade?

9. What did Len and Gary steal from Bill Webster's yard?

10. Whose nose did Gary Windass break in 2009?

For answers, please turn to page 136

The Ogdens

1 What was Hilda's maiden name?

2 Who gave the Ogdens their famous flying duck wall ornaments?

3 Which knight and ardent *Corrie* fan became Honorary Life President of the League for Hilda Ogden?

4 Why did Hilda dislike the occupant of 19 Inkerman Street?

5 What were the names of the Ogden offspring?

6 In a 1982 poll of the country's most recognisable women, where did Hilda rank?

7 Which Street couple once lodged with Hilda?

8 Prior to 1964, what was Stan's job?

9 What did Stan and Hilda give to their daughter Irma in 1965?

10 Two of Stan and Hilda's children, Sylvia and Tony, were never seen on screen. How was their absence from the family home explained?

11 What item did Hilda weep over – in what was described as one of *Corrie*'s most moving scenes ever – following Stan's death?

12 What happened to Hilda when she went to help her new employers tidy up at their retirement home?

13 What did Hilda sing on Christmas Day 1987, her last day on the Street?

14 Where had Eddie Yeats been before he began lodging with the Ogdens?

15 Why did Hilda and Stan change their house number?

16 What did the Ogdens win in 1977, thanks to Hilda's slogan: 'Be a mistress as well as a wife and your husband will be a boyfriend'?

17 What did Stan and Eddie clean in 1978 that they thought would net them a tidy sum, only to be badly let down?

18 What did Hilda once queue all night for?

19 Who sued the council after injuring their foot on a paving stone?

20 What was Irma's son called?

For answers, please turn to page 137

The Battersbys

1. Which Battersby was an ex-lap dancer, prostitute and cocaine addict?

2. Who pinched her bridal bouquet from outside Dev Alahan's shop?

3. Which Battersby went down on one knee in the Rovers to propose to her boyfriend in 2010?

4. Which famous pop group played at Les and Cilla's wedding reception?

5. Who was killed in a car accident while driving Les Battersby to hospital?

6. Who pretended to have skin cancer before running off with the money that people had raised for her?

7. Who raped Toyah?

8. Who did Leanne borrow money from to open a restaurant?

9. How much did Leanne borrow from Roger?

10. On discovering that the factory syndicate had won £25,000 on the lottery, which two Battersbys set up a bank account in Rosie Webster's name in order to claim the cash and keep it for themselves?

For answers, please turn to page 137

The Croppers

1. What was Hayley Cropper's name prior to her sex-change operation?

2. Later one of *Corrie*'s married women, who did the Croppers foster when she was a teenager?

3. Who tipped off the press on Roy and Hayley Croppers' wedding day, resulting in the planned service at the church being abandoned?

4. Where did the Croppers end up holding their commitment ceremony?

5. What was Hayley's maiden name?

6. What did Hayley do for Roy as a wedding present?

7. What was the name of the builder who bullied Roy in 2005?

8. Who did Hayley keep secret from Roy?

9. How did Hayley find her son?

10. Who did Roy call an ambulance for when he discovered him slumped outside the factory?

11 Which brash blonde did the Croppers befriend and employ to work at the cafe?

12 Where did Hayley work when she first appeared in the Street?

13 In an attempt to protect him from his stepfather, whom did the Croppers go on the run with?

14 The Croppers were godparents to which *Corrie* child?

15 Which country did Hayley go to as a volunteer aid worker between 2007 and 2008?

16 While volunteering, whom did Hayley develop a crush on?

17 Who did Roy buy his share of the cafe from in 1997?

18 Where did Hayley have her sex-change operation?

19 What kind of vehicles did Roy have a particular passion for?

20 What were Roy and Ken accused of doing by the police in 2008?

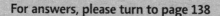
For answers, please turn to page 138

The Duckworths

1. Which Duckworth posed nude for a life-drawing class?

2. Which fellow factory worker was Vera best friends with?

3. Who was Vera convinced that she was related to?

4. Although she had a soft heart, Vera had a sharp tongue. For instance, who did she claim was: 'that hard faced, if she fell on the pavement she'd crack a flag'?

5. Finding out her husband Jack had been seeing Tina Fowler, how did Vera exact her revenge?

6. Opting for stone cladding, what colours did Jack and Vera choose for the 'fetching' exterior of chez Duckworth?

7. What was Jack's brother called?

8. Who became Jack's (platonic) lady friend after Vera's death?

9. Which Duckworth worked in an abattoir?

10. Who was the mother of Terry's son Paul?

11. Where did Jack and Vera meet?

12. What did Paul set fire to in 2008?

42

13 Who did Jack and Vera take in as a surrogate son?

14 Which of the Duckworth's lodgers got Vera a job at Betterbuys?

15 What property did the Duckworths buy in 1995?

16 Whose ghost did Vera think she was being haunted by?

17 How many grandchildren did Vera and Jack have?

18 How old was Vera when she died?

19 Jack was once part of a syndicate that bought a racehorse. What was the horse's name?

20 What did the Hortons 'buy' from Terry for £10,000?

For answers, please turn to page 138

The Websters

1. What was the name of Sally's sister?

2. What was the name of Kevin's sister?

3. Where did Kevin's father and sister move to, leaving Kev on the cobbles?

4. Which of her daughters did Sally try to push into stage school?

5. Which teacher did Sally develop a crush on in 2007?

6. What did Kevin do on the eve of his marriage to Alison Wakefield?

7. What did Kevin do on the day of Sally's marriage to Danny Hargreaves?

8. The body of whom did Kevin discover in the garage in 2005?

9. What did Sophie send to Norris Cole, leading him to believe that Sally had a crush on him?

10. In 2009, who started sharing the book-keeping for the garage with Sally?

11. When Kevin tried to break the news of his affair with Molly Dobbs to Sally, what news of her own did she break that stopped Kevin from spilling the beans?

12 Who did Bill Webster run off with soon after her marriage to Fred Elliott?

13 Which Webster provided *Corrie* with its first lesbian kiss?

14 What was the name of the private school attended by Rosie Webster?

15 Which Webster sister faked a pregnancy scare in a bid to grab her parents' attention?

16 Which member of the Webster clan was named after the street where they were born?

17 What style did Rosie adopt in 2004, goth or punk?

18 Who dated Craig Harris?

19 How did Kevin and Sally meet?

20 Who was Kevin's partner when he bought into the garage?

For answers, please turn to page 138

The Baldwins

1. How was Danny Baldwin related to Mike?

2. What was Danny Baldwin's wife called?

3. What was Mike's middle name?

4. Who owned Baldwin's Casuals?

5. Who did Jamie Baldwin leave Weatherfield with?

6. Which wannabe WAG did Warren Baldwin date?

7. What was Mike's dad called?

8. How many times was Mike married?

9. What were the names of Mike's wives?

10. How many children did Mike have?

11. What were the names of Mike's children?

12. How did Danny and Frankie Baldwin meet?

13. Who did Frankie begin a relationship with, causing a major stir on the Street?

46

14 Which Baldwin had a relationship with Underworld machinist Joanne Jackson?

15 What was the name of the florist that Mike had a relationship with?

16 What was the name of Danny's alcoholic ex-wife?

17 Who seduced and then blackmailed Mike in 1998?

18 Which Baldwin played football for Weatherfield County?

19 Who set Mike up to get caught drink driving?

20 Who was Danny's mother?

For answers, please turn to page 139

HOT POT LUCK

Quiz One

1. On what date was *Coronation Street* first screened?

2. Raquel Wolstenhulme, later Raquel Watts, once worked as a model. What was her 'model' name?

3. Who was proud of her unusual decorative 'muriel'?

4. Who suffered a nervous breakdown in 1992 and was found at the railway station wearing her slippers?

5. What medical procedure did Ashley Peacock have in 2009?

6. Who called himself Gerald Murphy when he joined an introductions agency, only to end up with his ex-fiancée as his date?

7. Later called *The Weatherfield Gazette*, what was the original name of the *Corrie* local paper?

8. What did Des Barnes set fire to when his wife Steph walked out on him?

9. Prior to transmission, what was *Corrie*'s working title?

10. What was the real name of the Harris family, who moved into the Street in 2002 when they were under the Witness Protection Programme?

For answers, please turn to page 139

Quiz Two

1 Which elderly resident of the Street was famous for her mauve hair and her passion for Percy Sugden?

2 Why did Weatherfield lose out on the prize at the French–English Meats competition?

3 Who did Cilla Battersby-Brown falsely accuse of giving her son Chesney brain damage as a result of a slap?

4 When Angela Griffin, Gaynor Faye, Jane Danson, Holly Newman and Tracy Shaw appeared on ITV's *Celebrity Stars in Their Eyes*, who did they appear as?

5 Actor Johnny Briggs (Mike Baldwin) attended which famous London stage school?

6 Who appeared as Britannia in the Christmas Day show staged by the residents in the pub in 1972?

7 Denise Osborne entertained the locals on karaoke night at the Rovers by singing which song?

8 What is taxi driver Lloyd's surname?

9 Who formed the WARP (Weatherfield Association of Ratepayers)?

10 On whose TV show did Tina McIntyre, Nick Tilsley, Graeme Proctor and David Platt appear, in character, in 2010?

For answers, please turn to page 140

Quiz Three

1 What was the name of Jerry Morton's eldest daughter?

2 Which chat show host once said: 'There was life before Coronation Street. But it didn't add up to much...'?

3 Who overcame his fear of flying to go on honeymoon, but then couldn't face the return trip and so hitched a ride on a trawler?

4 Which pop act was the actress Kym Marsh (Michelle Connor) formerly a member of?

5 Who were Arthur and Guinevere?

6 Who 'kidnapped' Arthur and Guinevere in 1995?

7 Who was Emily's bridesmaid when she married Ernest Bishop?

8 Who was interviewed on Radio Weatherfield about a UFO sighting?

9 Which pop act was Keith Duffy (Ciaran McCarthy) a member of?

10 Which *Corrie* actress was also famous for her *Results* series of fitness DVDs?

For answers, please turn to page 140

Quiz Four

1. Which former *Corrie* actress once appeared in a film with Morecambe and Wise?

2. Which ex-*Corrie* actor was a stuntman and also a founder member of the Society of British Fight Directors?

3. Who did Ken once describe in the paper as 'the debonair dynamo of denim'?

4. Who was shocked when his estranged wife returned to Weatherfield to tell him that he had a three-year-old daughter called Alice?

5. Which actress laid the foundation stone for the new outdoor lot, which was visited by the Queen in 1982?

6. Who was sent to Coventry for spreading gossip in 1961?

7. Which early character was a surreptitious gambler with a flair for picking winners?

8. Who played Buttons in the Rovers production of *Cinderella* in 1975?

9 Who had to have a piece of shrapnel removed from his bottom in 1975?

10 Who spent her inheritance from her late brother on new carpets and a bidet?

For answers, please turn to page 140

Quiz Five

1. What major purchase did Sally and Kevin make in 1988?

2. Terry Duckworth and who started up a removal business called Cheap and Cheerful?

3. What did Ivy Tilsley do to Martin Platt when she realised that he and Gail were an item?

4. Which brassy lady referred to almost everyone as 'cock'?

5. Craig Charles (Lloyd Mullaney) also starred in which cult TV show?

6. In 1961, 'bloody' was the first swear word uttered on *Corrie*. Who was the cursing character responsible?

7. Name all of Gail's husbands.

8. Which character developed a taste for Planter's Punch while working on a cruise ship?

9. Who did Stan buy his window-cleaning round from?

10. Which *Corrie* role did the actor who played I-Spy go on to play?

For answers, please turn to page 140

Quiz Six

1. The video for which chart-topping Queen song allegedly paid homage to *Corrie*?

2. In 1986, the closing credits for one particular episode were especially long. Why was this?

3. Which member of the royal family was reputed to be a regular viewer?

4. Who was Gordon Lewis?

5. Which Status Quo rockers appeared in four episodes of *Corrie* in 2005?

6. Who used a social networking site to try and track down his son in 2010?

7. Who recited 'The Owl and the Pussycat' at the Christmas party in 1969?

8. In which number Coronation Street did Betty Lawson and her family squat in the early 60s?

9. Which late lady novelist once wrote to a TV magazine on the subject of Elsie Tanner's love life?

10. What stage name did part-time stripper Sam Kingston adopt?

For answers, please turn to page 141

Quiz Seven

1. What displaced item in the Ogden house prompted a deluge of calls from listeners to Terry Wogan's breakfast show on Radio 2?

2. What did Blanche bequeath to grandson Simon in her will?

3. In an early episode, which character muddled his words and ended up saying: 'I don't know anything about history except King Harold riding about on his hawk a horse on his hand'?

4. Who was Vikram Desai's sister?

5. How was Vikram Desai related to Dev Alahan?

6. What nationality was the cleaner that Nick Tilsley and David Platt tried to bribe during their mum's trial?

7. Who once worked at Chuckles Novelties?

8. Which pensioner did the Platt children once use as a model for their Guy on bonfire night?

9. In 1973, who was caught underage drinking in the Rovers?

10. Who did Hilda Ogden accuse of being 'lax from the neck up and relax from the neck down' in 1969?

For answers, please turn to page 141

Quiz Eight

1. How was *Corrie* actress Sarah Lancashire's father involved in the Street in the early days?

2. In 1976, which two characters were found the worse for drink in the cellar of the Rovers after being trapped there all night?

3. Who did Angie Freeman have a night of passion with after too much red wine?

4. Who did fishmonger Bert Gosling take a fancy to in 1975?

5. Who claimed to have a 'magic' tree in his garden?

6. Why did Alf stop using the chauffeur-driven mayoral limo?

7. Who moved away from the Street in 1990 for the first time in 30 years?

8. In 1973, which two men battled to become the last mayor of Weatherfield?

9. Who was Johnny Webb?

10. Employed by Alec to work in the Rovers, what was Charlie Bracewell's talent?

For answers, please turn to page 141

RELATIONSHIPS

Marriages

1. Which *Corrie* couple tied the knot on screen just two days before Prince Charles and Lady Diana Spencer?

2. Whose wedding reception did Annie Walker leave because the best man began reading out saucy telegrams?

3. What was the name of the lady who became the second Mrs Alf Roberts?

4. Who did Des Barnes marry in 1998?

5. Who did Kevin Webster marry in January 2000?

6. In which year did Rita Littlewood wed Len Fairclough?

7. Who married Eunice Nuttall in 1981?

8. Which couple celebrated their ruby wedding anniversary with a bash at the Rovers in 1983?

9. How many times was Elsie Tanner married?

10. Who did Deirdre Barlow marry in 1994?

11. Which couple wed on 19 June 1992?

12. Why did Derek Wilton refuse to attend Ted and Rita's wedding?

13 Who did Liz MacDonald marry on New Year's Eve, 2007?

14 Who did Mike Baldwin marry on 10 September 2000?

15 Which couple married on 27 September 1991?

16 Who was threatened with a shotgun by his wife of just one week in 1991?

17 Which couple, often involved in comical storylines, were married on 26 January 1994?

18 What was wrong with the marriage between Emily Bishop and Arnold Swain?

19 Who married Robert Preston in 1996?

20 Which young couple eloped to Gretna Green in January 1998?

For answers, please turn to page 142

Flings, Flirtations and Affairs

1. While husband Ashley was laid up in hospital, Maxine Peacock had a fateful night of passion with which character?

2. Who had a fling with both Rita Littlewood and Bet Lynch in 1975?

3. Dev Alahan had a near-fatal relationship with a mad-as-a-box-of-frogs solicitor. What was her name?

4. Martin and Gail Platt's divorce was caused by his affair with colleague Rebecca who?

5. Sally Webster got up close and personal with Les Battersby's son. What was the name of Les's violent offspring?

6. Which killer schoolgirl did Martin Platt fall for?

7. Which barmaid – already embroiled in a fling with a married man – also managed to find time to seduce Des Barnes away from Raquel Wolstenhulme?

8. To whom was Deirdre Hunt briefly engaged in 1975?

9. Who had an affair with reporter Sally Waterman?

10. Who accused Curly Watts of sexual harassment in the workplace?

11 Who did Alec unwittingly snuggle up to in bed, thinking it was Rita – and how did the situation come about?

12 Who had an affair with Greg Kelly that descended into violence in 1998?

13 Who kissed Nick Tilsley while he was dozing, much to Nick's disgust?

14 Who had a dalliance with Walter Fletcher, a salesman, in 1961?

15 Nigel Havers played a male escort in 2010. What was his character's name?

16 Who did Linda Sykes have a fling with before marrying Mike Baldwin?

17 Which shopkeeper did Deirdre Barlow once sleep with?

18 Who did Ian Davenport once have a fling with?

19 Who did Kevin Webster start out pounding pavements with, only to end up cheating on his wife Sally with?

20 Which two characters were embroiled in *the* affair of 1983?

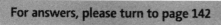
For answers, please turn to page 142

CHILDREN AND PETS

Babies

1. In 1990, which character made their *Corrie* debut by being born on Christmas Eve?

2. Who was the first baby to be born in *Corrie*?

3. Who gave birth to a baby boy in December 1980?

4. Before becoming parents themselves, Gary and Judy Mallett tried to buy the baby of a pregnant teenager. What was the name of the gymslip mother?

5. What did Roy and Hayley Cropper name Tracy Barlow's baby?

6. Who had a baby boy in the romantic setting of the back room of the pub on Valentine's Day 1997?

7. Born on Christmas Day 1998, what were Gary and Judy Mallet's twins called?

8. Who became the father of twins in 1965?

9. Who was born in February 2004?

10. Who were the parents of baby Sophie, born on 4 November 1994?

11. What did hairdresser Fiona Middleton name her baby son?

12 Who gave birth to baby Daniel in 1995?

13 Who was baby Shannon Tattersall's father?

14 Who was the mother of Tommy Duckworth?

15 Who was the father of Mark Redman, who was born in 1983?

16 Who was the father of Joshua Peacock?

17 Which baby was played by identical twins Jake and Oscar Hartley?

18 What was the name of Liam and Maria Connor's second baby?

19 Who were the parents of baby Dylan Wilson?

20 Which baby was born on 17 July 2006, resulting in a severe bout of post-natal depression for the tot's mother?

For answers, please turn to page 143

Our Kid

1. Which *Corrie* kid was briefly home-tutored by his sister?

2. The role of which child was played by Holly Bowyer, Rebecca Pike, Louisa Morris, Madison Hampson, Amber Chadwick and Elle Mulvaney?

3. Which little lad was being raised by his dead mother's husband and his new wife?

4. What were the names of Dev and Sunita Alahan's twins?

5. Which child had to endure his dad turning up drunk to the school nativity play?

6. Jesse Chadwick made his first appearance in *Corrie* as a children's entertainer for the birthday party of which tot?

7. Which child, originally named Thomas, had his name changed in memory of his late grandfather?

8. Which *Corrie* kid's middle name was Britney?

9. Which child was given the birth name Lauren, only to have it changed when her sibling persisted in calling her by a different name?

10. Which baby was born on a deserted beach?

For answers, please turn to page 143

Eh Up, Pet

1. What was the name of Minnie Caldwell's cat?

2. Emily Bishop once looked after Dolores, who was what type of animal?

3. What creature-inspired gift did Tyrone present Jack Duckworth with on the occasion of his 60th birthday?

4. In 1990, which much-loved pet found the shock of moving house too great and expired?

5. What did Tyrone call his beloved greyhound?

6. Which *Corrie* pet was recast in the late 80s?

7. What is the name of the dog that resided with the Barlows – a four-legged friend that was taken on a lot of walks by the canal when Ken was smitten with the owner of a houseboat?

8. Which of Rita's foster children had a dog named Mitzie?

9. Which couple and a dog fell through the bathroom ceiling while in a hot tub?

10. Who had a budgie called Randy?

11. Which Street residents kept chickens in their backyard?

12 Who had a cat called Marmaduke?

13 Which character had a pigeon called Gilbert?

14 Who owned a German shepherd by the name of Fury?

15 Theresa the turkey gobbled her last when which character killed her?

16 Who was thrilled when 'Freddie' the fox started visiting her garden?

17 What did Simon Barlow call his pet rabbit?

18 Don Brennan was once given a pregnant greyhound. What was it called?

19 In 1986 Hilda Ogden inherited a cat called what?

20 What was the name of the dog belonging to Judy and Gary Mallet?

For answers, please turn to page 143

DEPARTURES

Deaths

1. Which *Corrie* character died in 1961, having been run over by a bus?

2. Which parents were dealt a shocking blow in January 1992 when their baby girl, Katie, died the day after birth?

3. Who was stabbed and subsequently died outside a nightclub in 1989?

4. What did Alma die of?

5. Obsessed with Curly Watts, how did Anne Malone meet her maker?

6. How did Lisa Duckworth die?

7. Which of Deirdre's husbands died after being attacked while walking by the canal in 1995?

8. How did Des Barnes die?

9. Which character had a heart attack and died comfortably in his armchair on New Year's Day, 1999?

10. PC Emma Taylor shot and killed whose brother in a supermarket siege?

11 Which of Gail's grandchildren died the day after being born?

12 Who was killed in a car accident in 1983, on his way back from seeing a woman he was having an extramarital affair with?

13 Who died from a heart attack in the snug at the Rovers in 1964?

14 Whose husband, a former policeman, went to the great cop shop in the sky in 1974?

15 Who committed suicide after he admitted killing Steve Tanner?

16 How did Renee Roberts die?

17 Which of Rita's husbands died in 1992?

18 Which member of the Walker clan died suddenly in 1970?

19 Which character suffered the first Street death, in 1960?

20 What triggered Derek Wilton's fatal heart attack?

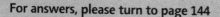 **For answers, please turn to page 144**

Murder!

1. In an episode steeped in bloodshed, who was Richard Hillman disguised as when he attempted to murder Emily Bishop and, when she walked in and saw what he was up to, killed Maxine Peacock?

2. Who arranged to have Liam Connor killed in a hit and run?

3. Who murdered builder Charlie Stubbs?

4. Which character confessed to the murder of his ex-wife, Patricia?

5. Which murder victim did Len Fairclough discover in his kitchen in 1975?

6. Who was charged with the murder of drug dealer Tony Horrocks?

7. Which of Hilda Ogden's employers died from a heart attack, brought on by a raid on her home?

8. Where was Brain Tilsley when he was fatally stabbed?

9 Who murdered her father by hitting him on the head with a monkey wrench and then later felt so guilty that she committed suicide?

10 How was Ernest Bishop, much-beloved husband of Emily, murdered at the factory?

For answers, please turn to page 144

Over and Out

1. Who did Hilda Ogden go to work for when she left the Street?

2. Which character left the cobbles for the more exotic location of Mexico?

3. Who left Weatherfield in 2005 to set up home with his ladylove in Liverpool, where they went on to have a baby daughter?

4. Where was Blanche Hunt holidaying when she died (the actress who played her, Maggie Jones, having died earlier in 2010)?

5. Who left the Street in tears after Nick Tilsley manipulated her into pinching financial details from Underworld?

6. After giving up on Martin Platt ever leaving wife Gail, Rebecca Hopkins handed in her notice at the hospital and headed for a new job in which country?

7. Where did Elsie Tanner go with Bill Gregory to run a bar?

8. Where was Florrie Lindley bound for when she left the soap in 1965?

9. Where were we to believe that Sarah Platt went to live?

10. Where did Curly, Emma and Ben Watts move to when they left Coronation Street?

11 Where did Ivy Tilsley go when she left the cobbles?

12 Which elderly male character left to live in a retirement complex called Mayfield Court?

13 Which female character also swapped the cobbles for the delights of Mayfield Court?

14 Where did Mavis go when she left the Street?

15 Which city did Dev Alahan's daughter Amber leave Weatherfield for, to attend university?

16 Who left the Street to go and run a supermarket in Lowestoft?

17 Who left the Rovers in 1983 to live with her daughter Joan, in Derby?

18 Whose exit saw her headed for St Anne's to look after her friend Henry Foster?

19 Whose promotion with Gamma Garments took him away from the Street in 1965?

20 Having admitted his homosexuality and almost been run out of town by his furious almost-mother-in-law Gail, where did Todd Grimshaw head for?

For answers, please turn to page 144

WEATHERFIELD

On the Map

1. What unimaginative name did Sally Webster and Danny Hargreaves give to their hardware store?

2. What was the name of the travel agency that Alec Gilroy managed?

3. Who once ran a baby linen shop in nearby Mawdsley Street?

4. Which character was associated with the address 5 Grasmere Drive, Oakhill?

5. Which streets bordered Coronation Street?

6. By what name was the recreation ground in *Corrie* better known?

7. What was the name of the cafe in the Street?

8. Who bought The Kabin in 2009?

9. Who purchased the hairdressing salon from Fiona Middleton?

10. Maxine Heavey set up a rival salon called A Cut Above with which other character?

11. Which business on the Street had previously been the Mark Brittain Warehouse and Elliston's Raincoats?

12 Who named their house The Old Rectory, believing a name to be classier than a number?

13 At which number Coronation Street did the Ogdens once reside?

14 On which road was the local supermarket located?

15 True or false: the cafe address was 12 Coronation Street?

16 Which hospital were infirm residents of the Street usually taken to?

17 Quarryman's Rest was a pub once offered to which Rovers landlord and landlady?

18 Who owned Valandro's restaurant?

19 What feature of the Street did residents protest about in 2000?

20 Which real-life street was the architecture of Coronation Street based on?

For answers, please turn to page 145

83

Tuck in, Lad!

1. What was Elsie Tanner's regular order in the Rovers?

2. Which Rovers character was famous for her hotpot?

3. What was Mike Baldwin's spirit of choice?

4. Which character once tried to bribe an official at a black pudding contest?

5. What was Ena Sharples' regular tipple?

6. Which redheaded lodger of Elsie Tanner's once accepted a modelling job promoting German sausages in a supermarket?

7. Who ran a bakery in Victoria Street between 2005 and 2006?

8. Who tried to spice up her marriage with the aid of parsnips, having heard that they boasted aphrodisiac qualities?

9. Who accused Alf Roberts of selling out-of-date Christmas puddings?

10. Who poured anti-freeze into one of the freezers at Firman's in a protest over Norwegian prawns?

11. What did Jerry Morton's food outlet specialise in?

12 What kind of fast-food joint did Cilla Battersby-Brown work in with Yana Lumb?

13 What was Eddie Windass's culinary talent?

14 What are the two key ingredients of hot pot?

15 Who was caught out when he tried to enter a vegetarian banger in a sausage-making contest?

16 What was wrongly blamed for an outbreak of food poisoning in the Rovers in the 90s?

17 The Clock and which other restaurant were frequently mentioned in *Coronation Street* over the years?

18 Which character loved a cuppa – and then read the tea leaves when she'd savoured the final drop?

19 What did Vera Duckworth once trick her husband into believing she had used as a filling for a home-baked pie?

20 What was Fred Elliot's usual drink?

For answers, please turn to page 145

By Numbers

1. The notching up of how many episodes did the Street celebrate on 15 April 1996?

2. How much money did Vera win from a night at the bingo in 1984?

3. In which year was the first hour-long special broadcast?

4. After appearing in a whopping 1,148 episodes, which character left the cobbles for good in 1980?

5. Which actress died in 1997 after 528 appearances in the Street?

6. Forty-nine thousand old what were sourced to help give *Corrie* an authentic look?

7. How much did Martin and Gail pay for 8 Coronation Street in 1991?

8. How many episodes did *Corrie* celebrate on 4 December 1989?

9. How many times was Gail married?

10. How old was Ken Barlow when he married Deirdre for the first time in 1981?

11. How many hours of community service did Les Battersby have to serve for defrauding the DHSS?

12 How many episodes a week began being transmitted in 1996?

13 An estimated 13.6 million viewers tuned in to see which character murder her boyfriend in 2007?

14 How many O levels did Curly Watts have?

15 By how many points did the Rovers lose in the Brainiest Pub Contest of 1985?

16 In which year did Alison Webster and Jez Quigley die?

17 What was notable about the Happy Hour at the Rovers in 1992?

18 How many viewers tuned in to see Richard Hillman confess his murderous deeds to Gail in 2003?

19 How many of the original cast members remained in 2010?

20 How many weeks was Deirdre in prison for in 1998?

For answers, please turn to page 146

What's My Line?

1 Ida Barlow worked in the kitchen at which hotel?

2 What did Des Barnes do for a living?

3 Which two characters started up the cab firm Street Cars?

4 Which character's jobs included personnel officer, teacher, taxi driver, cafe assistant and newspaper editor?

5 Who almost took a job as a pianist at a local strip club, but was stopped by his wife?

6 Whose first appearance in the Street was as a dancer in the Orinoco Club?

7 Who featured in episode one, when she arrived to take over the running of the corner shop?

8 Who, briefly, took a job as a pall-bearer in 1992?

9 Who arrived on *Corrie*'s cobbles in May 1966 and took a job at Elliston's PVC factory?

10 Which three characters opened The Graffiti Club in 1983?

11 Which entrepreneurial duo set up a pirate radio station?

12 Which original female character worked as the caretaker of the Glad Tidings Mission Hall?

13 Who was the first lollipop man on the Street?

14 Who took over Stan Ogden's window-cleaning round?

15 Who was once appointed Father Christmas at Betterbuys, only to be sacked for ticking the children off for asking 'Santa' for too much?

16 Whose diverse CV was backed up by a BA second class honours degree in English and History in 1961?

17 Who once worked as a salesgirl for Charm Cosmetics?

18 Which character was once deputy head of Bessie Street School?

19 Who was once a lorry driver and had an accident while delivering bananas?

20 What was Archie Shuttleworth's profession?

For answers, please turn to page 146

89

Any Road Up

1. Who passed her driving test in 1976 and bought a second-hand Rover from a dodgy pal of Eddie Yeats?

2. Which couple called their car 'The Woody'?

3. Who ran a garage for motorbike repairs under the viaduct?

4. Who had borrowed Mike's car to take a girl out in when it was vandalised?

5. What type of car did Vera Duckworth win in a magazine competition?

6. What kind of car did Audrey persuade Alf Roberts to buy?

7. Which character passed her driving test in 1965, but didn't drive again for almost 30 years?

8. Which character broke her ankle while banger racing?

9. Whose car was Jenny Bradley driving when she knocked Martin Platt over?

10. Whose car did Percy win in a raffle?

11. Who bought a 1959 Morris Minor and called her 'Annie'?

12 Who bought a Mini in 1996 so that his family could go on outings?

13 Which Harry drove a bus?

14 Which Webster bought a sassy sports car that Chesney then pinched and crashed?

15 Who acted as Mike Baldwin's chauffeur in 1988?

16 A Street coach-trip to the Lake District in 1969 ended in a crash. What was the cause of the accident?

17 Which couple once went on a cycling holiday on a tandem, but found the ride to the railway station so tiring that they dumped the bike with the station porter and gave up on pedal power?

18 In the 70s, whom did Billy Walker take as a partner in the garage he owned in Canal Street?

19 What was Kevin and Tyrone's garage called?

20 Which fancy car did Mike Baldwin drive?

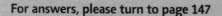**For answers, please turn to page 147**

Street Sports

1. Which contest did Stan Ogden win in the Pub Olympics of 1972?

2. What sport did Rovers landlord Duggie Ferguson play?

3. What kind of match did Sam Tindall play in a bid to woo Phyllis Pearce?

4. Set for a career as a professional footballer, what did David Barlow injure, putting paid to his ambition?

5. Which two golfers were both secretly taking private lessons in order to be a better player than the other?

6. What was replaced in the Rovers during *Corrie*'s early days when a viewer pointed out that the item in question was 'the wrong kind'?

7. Where, in 1964, did Stan Ogden wrestle Ian Campbell?

8. Who was the triumphant winner of the 1984 Pub Olympics egg and spoon race?

9 Who broke his leg on the golf course in 1997?

10 A viewer once contacted *Coronation Street* to draw attention to the fact that there was an out-of-date poster on display in the Rovers. What sporting event was the poster advertising?

For answers, please turn to page 147

COLOURFUL CHARACTERS

Bad 'Uns

1. With a voice that could strip wallpaper, who was poor Deirdre stuck with as a cellmate during her brief spell behind bars?

2. Who did Gail call 'Norman Bates with a briefcase'?

3. What was the name of the religious cult that Ben Andrews led?

4. Who did Tony Gordon try to evict by foul means?

5. Who did Charlie Stubbs almost succeed in drowning in a bath?

6. Who did John Stape kidnap?

7. What was killer Richard Hillman's profession?

8. What did Charlie Stubbs give to Shelley, only to viciously take back, causing her to shed blood?

9. Which crazy lady tried to kill Dev Alahan and Sunita Parekh?

10. Who got Roy Cropper drunk and convinced him that they had slept together and that he was the father of her unborn child?

11. A nasty piece of work if ever there was one, who was the result of a holiday romance between Moira Kelly and Les Battersby?

12 Who stole the deeds to Rita's house and impersonated her dead husband in order to try and take control of her money?

13 Which tie salesman stole Deirdre's heart, then her cash, and then stood by and let her take the blame for his numerous deceptions, the result of which condemned her to prison?

14 Which bent copper had it in for Becky McDonald?

15 Which GPO canteen worker conned Alf Roberts out of £500?

16 Posing as Mel Hutchwright, an author, what was the real name of the *Corrie* book club conman?

17 Who stalked PC Emma Watts then broke into her house, intending to attack her with a chisel?

18 Who led the gang of hoodies that raided the cafe and robbed The Kabin in 2008?

19 Which evil woman kidnapped Tyrone's beloved greyhound?

20 Whose henchman was Jimmy Dockerson?

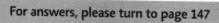

For answers, please turn to page 147

Battleaxes and Old Bags

1 Who was Maureen Holdsworth's grim and grumpy mother?

2 Which no-nonsense gravel-voiced pensioner had the hots for Percy Sugden?

3 Which waspish character left Ken Barlow her hardback Maeve Binchy books in her will?

4 Which redoubtable landlady regarded herself as superior to the rest of the Street's residents?

5 Who was Jack's battleaxe of a mother-in-law?

6 Which argumentative matriarch was at the centre of many rows and left the Street in 1994?

7 Which *Corrie* crone was almost never seen without her severe-looking hairnet?

8 Which battleaxe was played originally by Patricia Cutts?

9 Which confrontational female once had head lice and had to have her head shaved?

10 Who charmingly described his mother-in-law as 'Boris Karloff after a busy night at the graveyard'?

11 Which scheming Granny ran the corner shop for a time in the 70s?

12 Who insisted that all the Street's ladies withhold sexual favours from their menfolk in a row over a football bus?

13 Which trio were likened to the three witches from *Macbeth*?

14 Who celebrated her 90th birthday and being the oldest barmaid in Weatherfield in 2010, only to be challenged for the title of the latter by 91-year-old Enid Crump?

15 Which borderline bonkers competition-loving lady imprisoned Norris in a remote cottage in the country?

16 Which unlucky-in-love *Corrie* mother ran the office at Street Cars cab firm?

17 Which battleaxe met her match in Wally Banister – who fibbed about his wealth and then tried to chat up her granddaughter?

18 Which 'club' did Blanche Hunt and her friend May – no surname, just 'May' – attend, mixing with other elderly busybody biddies?

19 The characters Grishma and Upma Parekh were the interfering aunties of which character?

20 Which sweet-talking *Corrie* female once told Jodie Morton that she had 'the face of your father and the body of Jabba the Hutt'?

For answers, please turn to page 148

Sirens, Sex Symbols and Manchester Tarts

1. Which of TV's *Loose Women* was *Corrie*'s blonde bombshell?

2. Which flame-haired beauty lodged with Elsie Tanner and enjoyed flings with many chaps, including Mike Baldwin?

3. Which bride-to-be tried to cop off with a much younger man on her hen night, and when caught in her undies by the groom, passed the young buck off as her son, Billy?

4. Which dumb blonde inadvertently asked Ken Barlow if he would like to sleep with her – and how did this error occur?

5. She was embroiled with Alan Howard, Dan Johnson and Wilf Stockwell and enjoyed a long-term flirtation with Len Fairclough too. Who was this Street siren?

6. Which bitchy barmaid dated Des Barnes while he was involved with Raquel Wolstenhulme and then pinched Charlie Whelan from Bet Lynch?

7. Which barmaid and tart-with-a-heart, famed for her low-cut necklines, once had a fling with Jack Duckworth?

8. Which raven-haired widow was filmed cheating on her man by minxy Rosie Webster?

9 Which *Corrie* lady made her first appearance as an exotic dancer?

10 Which flighty lady seduced her teacher and was talked out of breast enlargements by her father?

11 Who was crowned Miss Petrol Pump in 1968?

12 Which brazen hussy slept with both a *Corrie* father and son, Mike and Mark Baldwin, in the 90s?

13 Which Battersby slept with both Danny and Jamie Baldwin?

14 Who had a one-night-stand with Toyah Battersby's boyfriend, then, when she fell pregnant as a result, claimed that Toyah's fella had raped her?

15 Who tried to stop Liam Connor from marrying Maria Sutherland because she wanted him for herself?

16 Who cheated on hubby Vernon with a married man?

17 Which Webster had sex with their boss in return for well-paid 'overtime'?

18 Who had a secret night of passion with Dev Alahan, which she only revealed a year later when her daughter began dating Dev?

19 Which floozy once tried to seduce only-gay-on-the-Street, Sean Tully?

20 Which voluptuous female, who once lived above the corner shop, flirted outrageously with shopkeeper Alf Roberts simply to wind him up, but was thoroughly shocked when he turned the tables and played her at her own game?

For answers, please turn to page 148

Staff and Landlords at the Rovers

1 Who were the landlords of the Rovers when *Corrie* was first broadcast?

2 In 2000, which landlady hung up her last pint mug before leaving the show on New Year's Eve?

3 What was the name of the barmaid who left the cobbles in 1988 and who went on to star in *Brookside*?

4 The Rovers Return was named in honour of Lieutenant Philip who?

5 Appearing between 1993 and 1994, Eva Pope played which beautiful but conniving barmaid?

6 Who was the first of *Corrie*'s barmaids?

7 Which triumvirate of local businessmen bought the Rovers in 2001?

8 Which couple bought the Rovers in 1995?

9 What was Fred Gee's job at the Rovers?

10 Which landlady once said: 'I'm not pulled as easy as a pint of Newton and Ridley's'?

11. Who won Newton and Ridley's 'Personality of the Pub' competition in 1975?

12. Who did barmaid Concepta Riley marry in 1961?

13. Which actress used to run her own pub in Cheshire, thus was perfectly at home playing a *Corrie* barmaid?

14. Which barmaid attracted the special attention of Jack Duckworth in 1989?

15. What was the surname of the pub's Welsh housekeeper Megan, who took up the post in 1989?

16. Which Rovers manageress became agoraphobic?

17. Which landlord locked Dan Mason in the cellar?

18. Which part-time *Corrie* barman delivered his baby son in the Rovers?

19. Which barmaid was involved in an incredible baby-swap storyline, which saw her meeting her 'real' son?

20. Which Rovers landlord was conned by Stacey, a canny lass who posed as Orchid, a Thai bride?

For answers, please turn to page 149

Nicknames

1. How was Norman Watts better known?

2. Fond of giving his staff nicknames, what did Danny Baldwin call Janice Battersby?

3. And what nickname did Danny give to Kelly Crabtree?

4. And what nickname did Danny pin on Sean Tully?

5. Whose CB radio handle was 'Slim Jim'?

6. Who was behind the CB radio handle 'Stardust Lil'?

7. By what name was Emily's nephew Geoffrey better known?

8. What did Jim McDonald always call Alec Gilroy?

9. Which character did Norris persist on calling Dirk?

10. Who did the media nickname 'The Weatherfield One'?

For answers, please turn to page 149

BEHIND THE SCENES

Back Street Boys and Girls

1 What was Eric Spear's contribution to *Corrie*?

2 Daran who was the show's official archivist for many years?

3 Adele Rose was the Street's longest-serving writer, with more than 450 scripts to her credit. Which popular children's TV drama did she go on to create for the BBC?

4 His first job at *Corrie* was as a senior cameraman, but he went on to become executive producer. Who was he?

5 Who created *Coronation Street*?

6 Which role was *Corrie*'s creator Tony Warren asked to cut, as it was believed that no actress could be found to do justice to the part?

7 Which producer caused shockwaves in 1997 when he culled a host of characters from the show, including Derek Wilton, Percy Sugden, Maureen Holdsworth and Andy McDonald?

8 What was Geoffrey Lancashire's job on Coronation Street?

9 Which critically acclaimed author of plays such as *Bar Mitzvah Boy* started his career writing for *Corrie*?

10 Who was script editor when *Corrie* began?

For answers, please turn to page 149

Awards, Accolades and Honours

1. Which long-serving Street actress was awarded an MBE in the New Year's Honours List in 2000?

2. Which *Corrie* actor won the prestigious Best Newcomer Award at the National Television Awards in 2010?

3. Which *Corrie* actress won Sexiest Female at the British Soap Awards in 2009?

4. Who won Most Popular Newcomer in 1995 at the inaugural National Television Awards?

5. Who won Best Soap Actress at the 2007 TV Quick Awards?

6. Russell Harty, Michael Parkinson and Willis Hall launched the British League for which character?

7. Who won the award for Sexiest Male at the British Soap Awards in 2006?

8. Who won Villain of the Year at the 2003 British Soap Awards?

9 What honour was bestowed on *Corrie* creator Tony Warren in 1994?

10 Who won the Royal Television Society Performance Award in 1985?

For answers, please turn to page 150

The Weatherfield Wardrobe

1. Which character got hitched wearing a charity shop frock and Dr Martens?

2. What kinds of garments were made at the factory when Tony Gordon was at the helm?

3. What kind of print did Bet Lynch/Gilroy favour?

4. Which character was often seen sporting a red anorak?

5. On account of her wearing glasses, which character was nicknamed 'Sexy Specs' by some of the tabloid newspapers?

6. How many (visible) curlers were worn by Hilda Ogden?

7. Who had a T-shirt emblazoned with the slogan: I've made gravy under shellfire?

8. Whose knickers were flown from a flagpole in 1980?

9. Which actress was regularly sent earrings by fans?

10. What was on the chain that Becky McDonald usually wore around her neck?

For answers, please turn to page 150

CAST

Bobbing In – Famous Visitors Quiz One

1. Who did Arthur Lowe of *Dad's Army* fame play in *Corrie*?

2. Bill Maynard once played a music agent on the Street. What was the name of the character he played?

3. Sir Ian McKellen, a proud *Corrie* fan, made a series of guest appearances in 2005 as which character?

4. Which member of which pop act played Len Fairclough's son Stanley: Herman of Herman's Hermits or Fred of Right Said Fred?

5. True or False: Mollie Sugden once played Annie Walker's friend Nellie Harvey?

6. Which Richard once played a *Corrie* copper who arrested Ena Sharples?

7. Which funnyman was cast as Archie Shuttleworth?

8. Although he never appeared on screen, which film director once posed for photographs at the bar of the Rovers?

9 Which musical theatre star appeared briefly as Malcolm Nuttall, a posh tennis-playing rival-in-love of Kevin Webster?

10 Douglas Wormold was a character who appeared briefly on the Street in the 70s. Which Michael played Douglas?

For answers, please turn to page 150

Bobbing In – Famous Visitors Quiz Two

1. Which Academy Award winner played Ron Jenkins in 1966?

2. Which member of the royal family made an appearance in the Street's 40th anniversary episode?

3. Which Tony has visited the Rovers: Blair or Christie?

4. Which comic actor played Ernie Crabbe in 2004?

5. Who was the love interest of Stephanie Beacham's character, Martha?

6. Which 'professional' man made an appearance as hippy Robert Croft in the 60s?

7. Comedian Peter Kay appeared briefly in 2004 as Eric Gartside and dated which *Corrie* lady?

8. Famous for playing Tanya Tucker in *Footballer's Wives*, Zöe Lucker played which character in 1996?

9. Which Academy Award winner had a brief role as a stroppy staff nurse in January 1977?

10. The Monkees' Davy Jones played Edna Sharples' grandson. What was his character's name?

11 Who once appeared in *Corrie* in a scene with his back to the camera, upon which were emblazoned the words 'Rock and Roll'?

12 Joanna Lumley played Elaine Perkins back in the early 70s. Whose girlfriend did she play?

13 Which former Bond girl played Rula Romanoff, a foxy lady who shocked Rita Sullivan and Norris Cole by suggesting they join the swinging scene?

14 Members of which rock group appeared in four episodes in 2005?

15 Which theatrical knight was keen to make a cameo appearance in a scene with Annie Walker, but whose schedule prevented him from ever doing so?

16 Which theatrical impresario and football club chairman played Gordon Clegg?

17 Which funnyman played Harry Payne, one of Elsie Tanner's many admirers?

18 Who appeared as bus conductress Eileen Hughes?

19 Who played Ramsay Clegg, Norris Cole's brother?

20 Who said: 'Tell me, where is the real Coronation Street'?

For answers, please turn to page 151

Life After *Corrie*

1. Tina Hobley briefly played barmaid Samantha Failsworth. Which medical TV show did she go on to star in?

2. Thelma Barlow, alias Mavis Wilton, went on to star in which Victoria Wood hit comedy series?

3. From the cobbles to the wilds of West Yorkshire, which long-running sitcom did Jean Alexander join when she took out Hilda's curlers?

4. As well as singing and modelling, what did Nick Tilsley actor Adam Rickitt try his hand at when he left the Street?

5. Who died on the cobbles and then joined the cast of another (albeit short-lived) soap opera?

6. Which *Corrie* actress went on to forge a name for herself in a multitude of TV shows, including *Clocking Off* and *Rose and Maloney*?

7. What role did *Corrie*'s Eddie Yeats play in TV's *Keeping Up Appearances*?

8. Which talented *Corrie* singer-songwriter won *Soapstar Superstar* in 2006?

9 Meg Johnson went from *Corrie* to *Brookside*, and then on to *Emmerdale* to play the part of Pearl Ladderbanks. Which character did she play in the Street?

10 Which actress and former Rovers barmaid went on to voice a character in the Wallace and Gromit film *A Matter of Loaf and Death*?

For answers, please turn to page 151

SPIN-OFFS, SPECIALS AND MEMORABLE MOMENTS

Street Fighting

1. Which bully sent a mob to give Steve McDonald a good kicking?

2. Which two *Corrie* ladies had a street catfight in which one of them was wearing only her dressing gown?

3. Who did Rosie Webster start brawling with at Jason Grimshaw and Tina McIntyre's housewarming party?

4. Who did bride-to-be Karen threaten with the heel of her wedding shoe?

5. Whose first appearance saw him arguing with Mike Baldwin about moving his car and, when Mike refused, lifted Mike's Jaguar up with a JCB?

6. Which raunchy character gave Lucille Hewitt a black eye in 1966?

7. Who was sent to prison for beating up John Stape?

8. Who did Claire Peacock call names and end up fighting with on the Red Rec?

9. Who did Liz McDonald throw out of the Rovers in a feud over Lloyd Mullaney?

10. Who did Elsie Tanner row in public with, accusing her of writing nasty anonymous letters?

For answers, please turn to page 151

Calamity *Corrie* – Disasters!

1. What was Don Brennan trying to do when he lost his leg?

2. How did bad girl Tracy Barlow almost die in 1995?

3. In 1986, whose attempts at mending the electrics resulted in a major fire at the Rovers, almost claiming the life of Bet Lynch?

4. What caused Molly and Tyrone Dobbs' terrible car accident?

5. How did Joe McIntyre die?

6. Who was rushed to hospital, having swallowed an Ecstasy tablet in 2007?

7. Which early Street character became trapped when the viaduct collapsed?

8. Who fitted the faulty gas fire that was responsible for almost killing Rita Sullivan?

9. Who got herself into serious danger with a character she met in an Internet chat room?

10. Which *Corrie* baddie met their maker when they were mown down by a tram in Blackpool in 1989?

11. Who drove Gail Hillman, her children Sarah and David and granddaughter Bethany into the canal?

12 Who suffered concussion after being hit by a black cab in London in 1973?

13 Who suffered a broken pelvis as a result of a coach crash in 1969?

14 Who was crushed to death when the jack collapsed while he was under Len Fairclough's van?

15 Who tried to poison Jerry Morton?

16 Who was left in a coma after agreeing to get into a car with Aidan Critchley?

17 Who was shocked and roundly humiliated by his girlfriend when, in an act of revenge for his infidelity, she unveiled a massive poster of him, naked, with the word 'LIAR' printed on it?

18 What did Jerry Morton suffer in 2008?

19 When John Stape kidnapped Rosie Webster, where did he keep her imprisoned?

20 Who did Bet Lynch prevent from taking an overdose on New Year's Eve, 1991?

For answers, please turn to page 152

Spin-off Sensations

1. What was the spin-off DVD starring Hayley, Roy and Becky called?

2. Who were the characters in *Romanian Holiday* supposed to be house-sitting for?

3. Which family featured in the spin-off DVD *Out of Africa*?

4. Which couple starred in the *Corrie* spin-off *Viva Las Vegas*?

5. *Pardon the Expression* was a spin-off TV series that focused on which *Corrie* character?

6. Six special episodes of *Coronation Street* were produced in the late 90s, following the storyline that took Steve and Vicky McDonald, Bet Gilroy, Reg Holdsworth and Vikram Desai to Brighton. Later released on video, what was the umbrella title given to these episodes?

7. What was the *Corrie* dance DVD released in 2004 called?

8. Which actor starred in a *Corrie* quiz DVD?

9 Which *Corrie* actress released a fitness DVD called *Dance it Off*?

10 What was the name of the video released in 1995 to celebrate the Street's 35th anniversary?

For answers, please turn to page 152

126

Unhappy 50th Birthday – Trial and Terror

1 True or false: Two possible outcomes to Gail McIntyre's trial were filmed.

2 Small-talk in the gallery between Mary Taylor and Norris Cole at Gail's court cast brought a lightness of touch to otherwise tense proceedings. What, for instance, did we learn that Mary had once queued for three days to buy, at a bargain price of £10.00?

3 Paul Dockery played a Crown Court clerk during Gail's trial. What was his real-life profession?

4 How much was the stake that Mary and Norris bet on the verdict?

5 In giving evidence, what did Gail tell the court Joe McIntyre's last words were?

6 Why was Tracy Barlow in hospital after Gail's trial?

7 How was the week of explosive episodes that saw Tony Gordon breaking out of jail known?

8 What was the name of Tony Gordon's cellmate and partner in crime in the Underworld siege?

9 Who played Robbie Sloan?

10 Which *Vicar of Dibley* character was James Fleet better known as?

11 What did Robbie say his line of business was in order to gain access to Underworld?

12 Behind which Charles Dickens book was the illegal mobile phone hidden for Tony in the prison library?

13 How did Tony acquire a SIM card?

14 What excuse did Carla Connor give to Bill Webster and Jason Grimshaw to stop them fixing the roof and to get them away from the factory while Tony had a gun trained on her?

15 Who did Tony Gordon kill during the factory siege?

16 Who walked in on Tony while he was holding Hayley Cropper and Carla hostage – and managed to walk away unhurt?

17 What did Carla hit Tony with when she had managed to free herself from her bonds?

18 Why were the factory siege episodes postponed, being screened a week after they were scheduled for transmission?

19 Where did Carla go with Trevor to recover from her ordeal at the factory?

20 On 31 May 2010 an overhaul of the opening sequence meant that Corrie could then be shown in what?

For answers, please turn to page 152

ANSWERS

CORRIE THROUGH THE YEARS

1960s

1. Florrie Lindley
2. Ken Barlow
3. Elsie Tanner
4. Dennis Tanner
5. Her son, Billy
6. Coronation Street was under threat of being renamed Florida Street by Weatherfield Council and she wanted him to intervene
7. Jack and Annie Walker
8. Len Fairclough
9. Minnie Caldwell
10. Hilda Ogden
11. An unexploded bomb
12. Charlie Moffitt, whose deception was discovered when Minnie and Emily tried it and got drunk rather than perky!
13. Emily Nugent
14. His brother David
15. Ray Langton
16. The Masked Lady
17. She had found a painting of a mystery lady in the pub's cellar, behind which a mask was concealed
18. November 1969
19. His coin collection
20. Effie Spicer

1970s

1. Bet Lynch
2. Betty Turpin
3. Ena Sharples
4. Mavis Riley
5. He watered down the gin in the Rovers
6. Betty Turpin
7. The Ogdens
8. Deirdre Hunt
9. Rita Littlewood
10. The Rosamund Street betting shop

11. Emily Bishop

12. Mavis Riley

13. A firework display

14. Mavis Riley

15. A pram race

16. His birth mother, Bet Lynch, who had given him up as a baby

17. Gail Potter

18. Blanche Hunt

19. Renee Bradshaw

20. Ivy Tilsley

1980s

1. Rita Fairclough

2. Her mother, Audrey

3. Arnold Swain, Emily's bigamous and mentally unstable husband

4. Eddie Yeats and Marion Willis'

5. Victor Pendlebury

6. To reveal the outcome of the Ken, Deirdre and Mike love triangle, which was scheduled for the same night that Manchester United played Arsenal. At 8 p.m. the board lit up with the words: Deirdre and Ken united again!

7. Peter Adams (Len Fairclough)

8. Deirdre Barlow

9. Kevin Webster

10. Jumpsuits

11. Ken Barlow, who took exception to the fact that Mike had proposed marriage to his daughter Susan

12. Alec Gilroy

13. Alf Roberts

14. Tom Casey

15. An artist on Alec Gilroy's books, she was an exotic dancer who performed with a troupe of budgerigars

16. Audrey Roberts

17. Mike Baldwin

18. Ken Barlow, who had been giving more than just dictation to Wendy Crozier

19. Mavis Riley and Emily Bishop

20. The McDonalds

1990s

1. Des and Steph Barnes

2. Ken Barlow

3. Tracy Barlow

4. Steph Barnes

5. Reg Holdsworth

6. A trip for two to Holland

7. Her shopping bag split, causing Percy to slip on some apples and break his ankle

8. Sarah Lancashire (Raquel Watts)

9. Don Brennan

10. A telescope

11. Don Brennan

12. Sarah Platt

13. Deirdre Barlow

14. Vicky Arden

15. Liz, Andy and Jim McDonald

16. Deirdre, when she was wrongly banged up for Jon Lindsay's crimes

17. Toyah Battersby

18. Jackie Dobbs

19. Alec Gilroy

20. Because he caught her eating a bacon butty

2000s

1. Sarah Platt and her pregnancy at the age of 13

2. Leanne Battersby

3. Natalie Barnes' sister Debs

4. Gary Mallett

5. Tyrone spray-painted graffiti on all the walls Les had just cleaned as part of his community service

6. Rita Sullivan

7. Amy – Dev proved she was a liar by ripping off the bandages from her wrists, which showed no sign of a suicide attempt

8. Karen McDonald

9. Marcus Dent

10. Ed Jackson, the man, unbeknown to Eileen at first, who many years before had shot Ernest Bishop in the factory raid

11. That her old school friend Paula Carp had had a relationship with her dad and that she had a half-sister, Julie

12. Jed Stone

13. Shelley Unwin

14. Tracy Barlow

15. Eileen Grimshaw

16. Violet Wilson

17. Jimmy Dockerson

18. Tony Gordon

19. Rita Sullivan

20. George and Eve Wilson, Simon's maternal grandparents

WHO'S WHO?

Quiz One

1. Elizabeth Dawn
2. Johnny Briggs
3. Graeme Proctor
4. Bill Tarmey
5. Vicky Binns
6. Doris Speed
7. Sophie
8. Steve Jackson
9. Jean Alexander
10. Jimmi Harkishin

Quiz Two

1. Shobna Gulati
2. Deirdre Barlow
3. Chris Gascoyne
4. Leanne Battersby
5. Chesney Battersby-Brown
6. Julie Carp
7. Hayley Cropper
8. Eileen Grimshaw
9. Ciaran McCarthy
10. Katherine Kelly

Quiz Three

1. Liz McDonald
2. Rita Sullivan
3. Andrew Whyment
4. Steve McDonald
5. Tina McIntyre
6. Roy Cropper
7. Alan Halsall
8. Eileen Derbyshire
9. Jack Howarth
10. Nigel Pivaro

Quiz Four

1. Ken Barlow
2. Betty Driver
3. Deirdre Barlow
4. Gail McIntyre
5. Audrey Roberts
6. Michael Le Vell
7. Sally Whittaker
8. Norris Cole
9. Fred Elliott (I say, Fred Elliott!)
10. Janice Battersby

Quiz Five

1. Sally Lindsay
2. Tracy Barlow
3. Cilla Battersby-Brown
4. Brooke Vincent
5. Chesney Battersby-Brown

6. Mark Redman
7. Jon Lindsay
8. Peter Adamson
9. Florrie Lindley
10. Derek Wilton

Quiz Six

1. Penny King
2. Fiz Stape
3. Tina O'Brien
4. Susie Blake
5. Jamie Baldwin
6. Rosie Webster
7. Jack P. Shepherd
8. Sean Tully
9. Tracie Bennett
10. Ryan Thomas

Quiz Seven

1. Ashley Peacock
2. Julia Haworth
3. Les Battersby-Brown
4. Julie Hesmondhalgh
5. Jenny Platt
6. Danny Baldwin
7. Tupele Dorgu
8. Samia Ghadie
9. Diggory Compton
10. Frankie Baldwin

HAPPY FAMILIES

The McDonalds

1. Andy
2. 11
3. Derek, a Newton & Ridley brewery deliveryman
4. Vicky Arden
5. He was convicted of receiving stolen alcohol
6. 2006
7. Fiona Middleton
8. Karen Phillips
9. Amy Barlow's
10. Steve McDonald
11. Steve and Andy
12. Liz – although Steve owned the pub, he couldn't be the licensee because he had a criminal record
13. Jim
14. Steve
15. Shania turned out to be a fella!
16. Harry Mason
17. Andy
18. Steve
19. Her ex-boyfriend Slug
20. Jim McDonald, who was furious that Vernon was marrying his ex-wife Liz

The Platts and the Tilsleys

1. Granny (Bethany's father was Brenda's son Neil)
2. Brian Tilsley
3. 1997
4. Ted Page
5. Sophie Webster
6. Bert
7. Martin Platt
8. Mechanic
9. Alma's
10. Audrey Roberts
11. Nick Tilsley
12. Stephen
13. Because Gail had had an affair with Brian's cousin Ian before she became pregnant
14. Don Brennan
15. David
16. Prescription painkillers
17. David
18. Sarah
19. Todd Grimshaw
20. Nick

The Barlows

1. David Barlow
2. Sally Waterman
3. 1981
4. She was run over by a bus
5. Frank
6. Deirdre
7. Martha, played by Stephanie Beacham
8. Denise Osborne
9. Mike Baldwin
10. Lucy Carmichael
11. Tracy. Samir was married to Deirdre Barlow, Tracy's mother, at the time
12. Blanche Hunt
13. Charlie Stubbs
14. Mike Baldwin
15. Aidan Critchley
16. Mike Baldwin
17. Shelley Unwin
18. Prince Charles and Camilla Parker Bowles
19. Tracy
20. Peter Barlow

The Windasses

1. Eddie
2. Anna
3. Joe McIntyre
4. Audrey Roberts

5. Eddie

6. Gary

7. Gary

8. Joe McIntyre's

9. Copper piping

10. David Platt's

The Ogdens

1. Crabtree

2. Hilda's Aunt Aggie – they were a wedding gift

3. Sir John Betjeman

4. She was Stan Ogden's bit on the side

5. Trevor, Irma, Sylvia and Tony

6. Fourth – behind the Queen, the Queen Mother and Diana, Princess of Wales

7. Kevin and Sally Webster

8. Lorry driver

9. A stake in the corner shop

10. They were put into care after they were beaten by a drunk Stan

11. Stan's spectacles

12. She was assaulted by burglars

13. 'Wish Me Luck as You Wave Me Goodbye'

14. In prison

15. They thought that the number 13 was bringing them bad luck, so they changed it to 12A. However, they were ordered by the council to change it back

16. A second honeymoon

17. The stained glass windows of St Margaret's Church – the vicar assumed they were doing it to be charitable!

18. To buy a cheap television in the January sales

19. Stan Ogden

20. Darren Barlow

The Battersbys

1. Leanne Battersby

2. Cilla Brown

3. Leanne, to Peter Barlow

4. Status Quo

5. Dennis Stringer

6. Cilla Battersby-Brown

7. Phil Simmonds

8. Roger Stiles, Janice Battersby's boyfriend

9. £10,000

10. Leanne and Janice

The Croppers

1. Harold
2. Fiz Brown
3. Les Battersby
4. Roy's Rolls
5. Patterson
6. She changed her name to Cropper by deed poll
7. Vince
8. Her son, Christian
9. She used the services of a private investigator
10. Tony Gordon
11. Becky Granger
12. Firman's Freezers
13. Wayne, a child placed in their foster care
14. Amy Barlow
15. Mozambique
16. Olaf, a project leader
17. Alma Baldwin
18. Amsterdam
19. Steam trains
20. Drug dealing

The Duckworths

1. Jack
2. Ivy Tilsley
3. The Queen
4. Natalie Barnes
5. She cut up all of his trousers
6. Yellow and blue
7. Clifford
8. Connie Rathbone
9. Terry
10. Andrea Clayton
11. The funfair – Jack was working on the waltzers
12. Valandro's restaurant
13. Tyrone Dobbs
14. Curly Watts
15. The Rovers Return
16. Ivy's
17. Three: Brad, Tommy and Paul
18. 70
19. Betty's Hot Shot
20. Their grandson, Tommy

The Websters

1. Gina Seddon
2. Debbie Webster
3. Southampton
4. Rosie
5. John Stape
6. He slept with Sally
7. He told Danny about his one-night-stand with Sally

8. Tommy Harris

9. A valentine card

10. Molly Dobbs

11. That she had cancer

12. Maureen Elliott

13. Sophie, when she kissed best friend Sian Powers

14. Oak Hill

15. Sophie

16. Rosie (Rosamund Street)

17. Goth

18. Rosie

19. Kevin drove through a big puddle and soaked her

20. Tony Horrocks

The Baldwins

1. Danny was Mike's nephew

2. Frankie

3. Vernon

4. Mike

5. Violet and her baby

6. Candice Stowe

7. Frank

8. Four

9. Susan Barlow, Jackie Ingram, Alma Halliwell and Linda Sykes

10. Three

11. Danny Baldwin, Mark Redman and Adam Barlow

12. Frankie was employed to babysit Danny's son Jamie

13. Jamie, her stepson

14. Jamie

15. Maggie Dunlop

16. Carol

17. Julia Stone

18. Warren

19. Ida Clough

20. Viv Baldwin

HOT POT LUCK

Quiz One

1. 9 December 1960

2. Nadia

3. Hilda Ogden

4. Emily Bishop

5. A vasectomy

6. Curly Watts

7. *The Recorder*

8. His boat

9. *Florizel Street*

10. Nelson

Quiz Two

1. Phyllis Pearce
2. Fred Elliott attempted to bribe the judges, which didn't go down too well!
3. Rita Sullivan
4. The Spice Girls
5. The Italia Conti Academy
6. Annie Walker
7. 'Fever'
8. Mullaney
9. Earnest Bishop
10. They appeared on *The Jeremy Kyle Show* so that Nick could take a lie detector test to prove he hadn't had sex with Tina!

Quiz Three

1. Jodie
2. Russell Harty
3. Ashley Peacock
4. Hear'Say
5. Garden gnomes belonging to Derek and Mavis Wilton
6. Norris Cole
7. Mavis Riley
8. Curly Watts

9. Boyzone
10. Beverley Callard

Quiz Four

1. Amanda Barrie (Alma Baldwin)
2. Brian Mosley (Alf Roberts)
3. Mike Baldwin
4. Curly Watts
5. Doris Speed (Annie Walker)
6. Ena Sharples
7. Minnie Caldwell
8. Len Fairclough
9. Albert Tatlock
10. Hilda Ogden

Quiz Five

1. 13 Coronation Street
2. Curly Watts
3. She hit him
4. Bet Lynch/Gilroy
5. *Red Dwarf*
6. Ken Barlow
7. Brian Tilsley, Martin Platt, Richard Hillman and Joe McIntyre
8. Hilda Ogden
9. I-Spy Dwyer
10. Alec Gilroy (Roy Barraclough)

Quiz Six

1. 'I Want to Break Free'
2. After the episode about the fire in the Rovers, a pigeon was caught on camera after the final sequence was filmed. Incredibly, it flew over the viaduct and settled on the charred Rovers sign. The credits were extended to include this God-given moment
3. The Queen
4. A useless relief manager at the Rovers who covered for Annie Walker in 1981
5. Francis Rossi and Rick Parfitt
6. Sean Tully
7. Minnie Caldwell
8. 3
9. Barbara Cartland
10. The Masked Python

Quiz Seven

1. One of Hilda's flying duck ornaments
2. A pocket watch
3. Frank Barlow, Ken's father
4. Nita
5. They were cousins
6. Polish
7. Derek Wilton
8. Percy
9. Tricia Hopkins
10. Her husband Stan

Quiz Eight

1. He was a writer on the show
2. Stan Ogden and Albert Tatlock
3. Curly Watts
4. Betty Turpin
5. Derek Wilton
6. He realised that Audrey had the hots for the chauffeur
7. Ken Barlow
8. Alf Roberts and Len Fairclough
9. A binman pal of Eddie Yeats who lodged with Eddie at the Ogdens for a while
10. He was a ventriloquist

RELATIONSHIPS

Marriages

1. Ken Barlow and Deirdre Langton
2. Eddie and Marion Yeats
3. Renee
4. Natalie Horrocks
5. Alison Wakefield
6. 1977
7. Fred Gee
8. Stan and Hilda Ogden
9. Three
10. Samir Rachid
11. Mike and Alma Baldwin
12. He believed Ted to be marrying Rita for her money; he did not realise that Ted was dying
13. Vernon Tomlin
14. Linda Sykes
15. Gail and Martin Platt
16. Mike Baldwin, who was briefly husband to feisty Jackie Ingram
17. Reg and Maureen Holdsworth
18. It was a bigamous marriage; Arnold was still married
19. Tracy Barlow
20. Leanne Battersby and Nick Tilsley

Flings, Flirtations and Affairs

1. Matt Ramsden
2. Len Fairclough
3. Maya
4. Hopkins
5. Greg Kelly
6. Katy Harris
7. Tanya Pooley
8. Billy Walker
9. Ken Barlow
10. Anne Malone
11. Betty Williams. Rita and Alec had connecting doors between their flats and Alec didn't realise that Betty was staying the night
12. Sally Webster
13. Todd Grimshaw
14. Elsie Tanner
15. Lewis Archer
16. Mike's son Mark
17. Dev Alahan
18. Sally Webster
19. Molly Dobbs
20. Deirdre Barlow and Mike Baldwin

CHILDREN AND PETS

Babies

1. Rosie Webster
2. Paul Cheveski
3. Gail Tilsley
4. Zoe Tattersall
5. Patience
6. Tricia Armstrong
7. William (Billy) and Rebecca (Becky)
8. Ken Barlow
9. Amy Barlow
10. Kevin and Sally Webster
11. Morgan
12. Denise Osbourne
13. Liam Shepherd
14. Lisa Duckworth
15. Mike Baldwin
16. Dr Matt Ramsden
17. Simon Barlow
18. Liam Junior
19. Violet Wilson and Sean Tully
20. Freddie Peacock

Our Kid

1. Chesney Battersby-Brown
2. Amy Barlow
3. Joshua Peacock
4. Aadi and Asha
5. Simon Barlow
6. Amy Barlow
7. Freddie Peacock (after Fred Elliott)
8. Beth Platt
9. Sophie Webster
10. Liam Connor

Eh Up, Pet

1. Bobbie
2. A donkey
3. One of Jack's recently deceased favourite pigeons, stuffed and mounted
4. Mavis and Derek Wilton's budgie, Harriet
5. Monica
6. The cat that featured in the opening credits
7. Eccles
8. Jenny Bradley
9. Les and Cilla Battersby-Brown and Schmeichel, the Great Dane
10. Percy Sugden
11. The Ogdens
12. Betty Williams
13. Albert Tatlock

14. Eddie Yeats
15. Les Battersby
16. Mavis Wilton
17. Leanne
18. Harry's Luck
19. Rommel
20. Scamper

DEPARTURES

Deaths

1. Ida Barlow
2. Jim and Liz McDonald
3. Brian Tilsley
4. Cervical cancer
5. She got trapped in a Freshco's freezer
6. She was hit by a car
7. Samir Rachid
8. He suffered a heart attack after being set upon by drug dealers
9. Alf Roberts
10. Linda Baldwin's
11. Billy (son of Sarah Platt and Todd Grimshaw)
12. Len Fairclough
13. Martha Longhurst

14. Betty Turpin's
15. Joe Donelli
16. In a car accident – she was thrown through the windscreen
17. Ted Sullivan
18. Jack
19. May Hardman
20. A road rage incident that occurred while he was driving

Murder!

1. Aidan Critchley
2. Tony Gordon
3. Tracy Barlow
4. Richard Hillman
5. Lynn Johnson, who had been killed by her husband
6. Jez Quigley
7. Joan Lowther
8. Outside a nightclub
9. Katy Harris
10. He was shot when the factory was robbed

Over and Out

1. Dr Lowther
2. Angie Freeman
3. Martin Platt

4. Portugal

5. Kelly Crabtree

6. Dubai

7. Portugal

8. Canada

9. Milan

10. Newcastle

11. She joined a convent and became a nun

12. Percy Sugden

13. Phyllis Pearce

14. To run a B & B in Cartmel in the Lake District

15. London

16. Reg Holdsworth

17. Annie Walker

18. Ena Sharples

19. Leonard Swindley

20. London

5. Viaduct Street and Rosamund Street

6. The Red Rec

7. Roy's Rolls

8. Norris Cole

9. Audrey Roberts

10. Tom Ferguson

11. Underworld

12. Vera and Jack Duckworth

13. 13

14. Albert Road

15. False. It was 12 Rosamund Street

16. Weatherfield General Hospital

17. Alec and Bet Gilroy

18. Leanne Battersby

19. The cobbles – Weatherfield Council was threatening to tarmac them

20. Archie Street in Ordsall, a district of Salford, which has since been demolished

WEATHERFIELD

On the Map

1. D & S Hardware

2. Sunliners

3. Emily Bishop

4. Audrey Roberts

Tuck in, Lad!

1. A gin and tonic

2. Betty Williams

3. Scotch

4. Fred Elliott

5. Milk stout

6. Suzie Burchall

7. Diggory Compton

8. Mavis Wilton

9. Percy Sugden

10. Toyah Battersby

11. Kebabs

12. Chip shop

13. Cake making

14. Lamb and potatoes

15. Ashley Peacock

16. Betty's hot pot. It was actually beer that was the real culprit

17. Delphine's

18. Hilda Ogden

19. One of his beloved pigeons

20. Scotch and threat (Scotch with just a drop – a 'threat' – of water)

By Numbers

1. 4,000

2. £250

3. 1995, for the marriage of Curly and Raquel Watts

4. Ena Sharples

5. Jill Summers, who played Phyllis Pearce

6. Bricks

7. £38,000

8. 3,000

9. Four

10. 42

11. 150

12. Four

13. Tracy Barlow (who dealt a killer blow to Charlie Stubbs)

14. Eight

15. One

16. 2000

17. It lasted an hour and a half!

18. 19.4 million

19. One – Ken Barlow

20. Three

What's My Line?

1. The Imperial Hotel

2. He was a bookmaker

3. Steve McDonald and Vikram Desai

4. Ken Barlow

5. Ernest Bishop

6. Rita Littlewood (later Rita Fairclough)

7. Florrie Lindley

8. Jack Duckworth

9. Bet Lynch

10. Len Fairclough, Mike Baldwin and Alf Roberts

11. Andy and Steve McDonald
12. Ena Sharples
13. Albert Tatlock
14. Eddie Yeats
15. Percy Sugden
16. Ken Barlow
17. Elsie Tanner
18. Ken Barlow
19. Stan Ogden
20. Funeral director

Any Road Up

1. Annie Walker
2. The Croppers
3. Jim McDonald
4. Terry Duckworth
5. Vauxhall Nova
6. MG
7. Emily Bishop
8. Sally Webster
9. Rita Fairclough's
10. Fred Gee's
11. Emily Bishop
12. Ken Barlow
13. Harry Hewitt
14. Rosie
15. Terry Duckworth
16. The coach had a problem with its steering

17. The Ogdens
18. Alan Howard
19. Webster's Auto Centre
20. Jaguar

Street Sports

1. Beer drinking
2. Rugby
3. Bowls
4. His knee
5. Dev Alahan and Steve McDonald
6. The dartboard
7. The Viaduct Sporting Club
8. Hilda Ogden
9. Fred Elliott
10. A boxing match

COLOURFUL CHARACTERS

Bad 'Uns

1. Jackie Dobbs
2. Serial killer Richard Hillman
3. The Etheric Foundation
4. Jed Stone
5. David Platt
6. Rosie Webster
7. Financial advisor

8. A pair of earrings – he ripped them from her ears
9. 'Mad' Maya Sharma
10. Tracy Barlow
11. Greg Kelly
12. Alan Bradley
13. Jon Lindsay
14. DC Hooch
15. Donna Parker
16. Lionel Hipkiss
17. Ryan Sykes
18. Kenzie Judd
19. 'Mad' Maya Sharma
20. Tony Gordon

Battleaxes and Old Bags

1. Maud Grimes
2. Phyllis Pearce
3. Blanche Hunt
4. Annie Walker
5. Amy Burton
6. Ivy Tilsley
7. Ena Sharples
8. Blanche Hunt
9. Janice Battersby
10. Jack Duckworth
11. Granny Hopkins
12. Annie Walker

13. Ena Shaples, Martha Longhurst and Minnie Caldwell
14. Betty Williams
15. Mary Taylor
16. Eileen Grimshaw
17. Blanche Hunt
18. The One O'clock Club
19. Sunita Alahan
20. Cilla Battersby-Brown

Sirens, Sex Symbols and Manchester Tarts

1. Denise Welch (Natalie Horrocks)
2. Suzie Burchill
3. Cilla Battersby
4. Raquel Wolstenhulme – Ken was teaching her French and she got in a tangle with the lingo, asking him: *'Voulez-vous coucher avec moi?'*
5. Elsie Tanner
6. Tanya Pooley
7. Bet Lynch
8. Carla Connor
9. Rita Sullivan
10. Rosie Webster
11. Audrey Bright
12. Linda Sykes

13. Leanne

14. Maria Sutherland

15. Carla Connor

16. Liz McDonald

17. Sally Webster (with garage owner Ian Davenport)

18. Deirdre Barlow

19. Kelly Crabtree

20. Bet Lynch

Staff and Landlords at the Rovers

1. Jack and Annie Walker

2. Nathalie Barnes

3. Gloria Todd

4. Ridley, the son of the family that owned the brewery

5. Tanya Pooley

6. Concepta Riley

7. Duggie Ferguson, Fred Elliott and Mike Baldwin

8. Jack and Vera Duckworth

9. Potman

10. Natalie Horrocks

11. Betty Turpin

12. Harry Hewitt

13. Betty Driver

14. Tina Fowler

15. Morgan

16. Shelley Unwin

17. Steve McDonald

18. Sean Tulley

19. Michelle Connor

20. Fred Elliott

Nicknames

1. Curly

2. Lippy

3. Legs

4. Mincemeat

5. Eddie Yeats

6. Marion Willis

7. Spider

8. Sandy

9. Derek Wilton

10. Deirdre Barlow

BEHIND THE SCENES

Back Street Boys and Girls

1. He wrote the legendary theme tune

2. Little

3. *Byker Grove*

4. Bill Podmore

5. Tony Warren

6. Ena Sharples

7. Brian Park

8. He was a scriptwriter

9. Jack Rosenthal

10. Harry Kershaw

Awards, Accolades and Honours

1. Betty Driver

2. Craig Gazey, who played Graeme Proctor

3. Michelle Keegan, who played Tina McIntyre

4. Angela Griffin, who played Fiona Middleton

5. Sue Cleaver, who played Eileen Grimshaw

6. Hilda Ogden

7. Richard Fleeshman, who played Craig Harris

8. Brian Capron, who played Richard Hillman

9. MBE

10. Jean Alexander, who played Hilda Ogden

The Weatherfield Wardrobe

1. Tracy Barlow (on becoming Mrs Preston)

2. Underwear

3. Leopard skin

4. Hayley Cropper

5. Deirdre Barlow

6. Three

7. Percy Sugden

8. Vera Duckworth's

9. Julie Goodyear (Bet Lynch)

10. A pendant spelling out her name

CAST

Bobbing In – Famous Visitors Quiz One

1. Leonard Swindley

2. Micky Malone

3. Mel Hutchwright

4. Herman of Herman's Hermits

5. True

6. Richard Beckinsale

7. Roy Hudd

8. Alfred Hitchcock

9. Michael Ball

10. Michael Elphick

Bobbing In – Famous Visitors Quiz Two

1. Sir Ben Kingsley
2. Prince Charles
3. Blair
4. Norman Wisdom
5. Ken Barlow
6. Martin Shaw
7. Shelley Unwin
8. Sonia Leach
9. Brenda Fricker
10. Colin Lomax
11. Sir Cliff Richard
12. Ken Barlow's
13. Honor Blackman
14. Status Quo (Francis Rossi and Rick Parfitt)
15. Sir Lawrence Olivier
16. Bill Kenwright
17. Max Wall
18. Prunella Scales
19. Andrew Sachs
20. The Queen

Life After *Corrie*

1. *Holby City*
2. *Dinnerladies*
3. *Last of the Summer Wine*

4. Politics – in 2005 he was approved as a prospective candidate for the Conservatives
5. Johnny Briggs (*Echo Beach*)
6. Sarah Lancashire (Raquel)
7. Onslow
8. Richard Fleeshman (Craig Harris)
9. Eunice Gee
10. Sally Lindsay (Shelley Unwin)

SPIN-OFFS, SPECIALS AND MEMORABLE MOMENTS

Street Fighting

1. Jez Quigley
2. Eileen Grimshaw and Gail Platt
3. Michelle Connor
4. Tracy Barlow
5. Charlie Stubbs
6. Bet Lynch
7. Kevin Webster
8. Janice Battersby
9. Teresa Bryant
10. Ena Sharples

Calamity *Corrie* – Disasters!

1. Commit suicide
2. Taking the drug Ecstasy
3. Jack Duckworth
4. Faulty brakes
5. He drowned
6. Bethany Platt
7. Ena Sharples
8. Steve McDonald
9. Sarah Platt
10. Alan Bradley
11. Richard Hillman
12. Elsie Tanner
13. Maggie Clegg
14. Harry Hewitt
15. His ex-wife Teresa
16. Sarah Platt
17. Dev Alahan
18. A heart attack
19. At his late grandmother's house
20. Ken Barlow

Spin-off Sensations

1. *Romanian Holiday*
2. Frankie Baldwin (while she was on honeymoon)
3. The Battersby-Browns
4. Jack and Vera Duckworth

5. Leonard Swindley
6. *The Rover Returns*
7. *Coronation Street Funk Fit*
8. Antony Cotton
9. Vicky Binns
10. *The Cruise*

Unhappy 50th Birthday – Trial and Terror

1. True.
2. A hostess trolley
3. A retired barrister
4. £5
5. 'I love you, Gail.'
6. Gail's cellmate and another prisoner beat Tracy up for being a grass
7. 'Siege Week'
8. Robbie Sloan
9. James Fleet
10. Hugo Horton
11. A market trader
12. *Martin Chuzzlewit*
13. It was given to him in place of a wafer during prison Holy Communion
14. That the insurance wasn't valid and so she wouldn't be able to pay them

15. Robbie

16. Maria Connor

17. The office chair that she had been tied to

18. Taxi driver Derek Bird went on a shocking and tragic killing spree the day the storyline was due to unfold. Producers deemed the *Corrie* events to be too similar to the horrendous events in Cumbria and thus the episodes were delayed

19. To South Africa for the World Cup

20. HD (high definition)

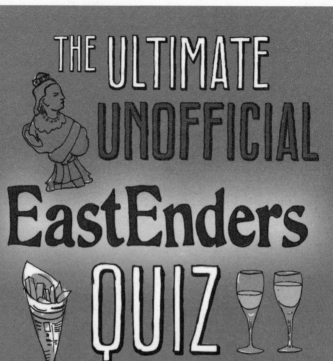

THE ULTIMATE UNOFFICIAL

EastEnders

QUIZ

BOOK

Ed Cobham

THE ULTIMATE UNOFFICIAL *EASTENDERS* QUIZ BOOK

Ed Cobham

ISBN: 978 1 84953 098 9   Paperback   £5.99

So you think you're one of *EastEnders'* biggest fans?
Test your knowledge with this trivia quiz book:

- **Where did Barry Evans propose to Natalie Price?**

- **What colour was the original exterior of the Queen Vic?**

- **Which character died in the middle of Albert Square on Christmas Day, 2006?**

If you think you're practically a resident of the Square, these brain-teasing questions will drive you Dotty until you've got them all!

BIGGEST
FASTEST
DEADLIEST

THE BOOK OF FASCINATING FACTS

DAN BRIDGES

BIGGEST, FASTEST, DEADLIEST
The Book of Fascinating Facts

Dan Bridges

ISBN: 978 1 84953 084 2   Hardback   £9.99

THE WORLD'S BIGGEST ISLAND:
Greenland, Arctic, 2,175,000 km² (840,000 m²)

THE WORLD'S FASTEST BIRD:
peregrine falcon, dives after prey at 124 mph (200 km/h)

THE WORLD'S DEADLIEST LAND ANIMAL:
golden poison frog of Central and South America

Ever wished you could remember everything you learned at school? Ever felt the answer to a tie-breaker was on the tip of your tongue? With this treasure trove of lists you can fascinate your friends with facts on astronomy, history, invention, the natural world and a wealth of other subjects.

Go on, dip in – there's still time to win *Mastermind*, or at least a round of Trivial Pursuit!

Have you enjoyed this book? If so, why not write a review on your favourite website?

Thanks very much for buying this Summersdale book.

www.summersdale.com